KU-496-934

Contents

Charlotte Keatley

1960 Born in London, 5 January.

1974 Won third prize in BBC Kaleidoscope Poetry Competition.

1979–82 Read Drama at Manchester University.

1980 *Sunday Times* Outstanding Performance Award for *The Raft of the Medusa* at the National Student Drama Festival. Acted at Edinburgh Festival with Manchester Umbrella Student Company in new plays by Ben Elton.

1981–82 Theatre critic for the *Festival Times, National Student Newspaper* and the *Glasgow Herald*, covering the Edinburgh Festival. Arts editor of *Mancunion Student Newspaper*, covering all theatre in the North West.

1981–85 Theatre critic for *Performance* magazine and Arts Editor of *National Student Newspaper*. Wrote numerous features and interviews with Pina Bausch, Akademia Ruchu, Anna Teresa de Keersmaker, People Show, Jan Fabre, Ivor Cutler, Steven Berkoff, Laurie Anderson, Max Wall, Taduez Kantor.

1982 Wrote and filmed a video at Bellevue, Manchester, about the closure of the traditional covered circus, one of the last two in England. Danced the Princess in Stravinsky's *A Soldier's Tale* for Manchester Camarata. Student production of *Underneath the Arndale* opened at Contact Theatre, Manchester, in June, directed by the playwright. Co-devised and performed *An American Childhood* with Impact Theatre.

1982–83 MA in Theatre Arts, Leeds University.

1983–87 Theatre critic for the *Yorkshire Post*, freelance.

1983 Student production of musical play *The Iron Serpent* at the Theatre Workshop, Leeds, in March, original score composed by Chris Moore, directed by Jon Barber, about the building of Manchester and the first public railway. Subsequently the play was given a rehearsed reading at the Royal Exchange Theatre in 1984.

1983–84 Co-devised and performed in *Dressing for Dinner* at the Theatre Workshop, Leeds. Selected for the Midland Arts Platform 1983.

1984–87 Theatre critic for the *Financial Times*, and for BBC
Kaleidoscope, freelance.

1985 Returned to Manchester to write. *My Mother Said I Never Should*
written in August and then entered for the Royal Exchange/
Mobil Playwriting Competition from which it was rejected.

1985–86 Applied for Arts Council Writers' Bursary at Padgate,
Warrington, rejected. Over the year wrote, directed and
designed a community play, working with over 300 people.
The Legend of Padgate, a mythic story of the earliest Anglo-
Saxon settlements in the area, with a rap chorus of masked
hogs, opened 8 June 1986, at Padgate Arts Centre, music by
Mark Vibrans, directed by the playwright. Re-applied for
Writers' Bursary in June 1986, again rejected.

1986 Rehearsed readings of *My Mother Said I Never Should* with
Paines Plough Theatre Company, London, and at North West
Playwrights' Workshop, Manchester.

1987 First production of *My Mother Said I Never Should* at Contact
Theatre, Manchester, 25 February, directed by Brigid
Larmour, winner of the *Manchester Evening News* Best New
Play Award, and joint winner of the 1987 Royal Court/
George Devine Award. *Waiting for Martin*, a monologue for
the mother of a soldier lost in the Falklands War, produced by
the English Shakespeare Company with *Henry IV*. Opened at
the Palace Theatre, Manchester, in March; and toured to the
Old Vic, London, and across Canada.

1987–88 Wrote ten of the first episodes of *Citizens* for BBC Radio 4,
first broadcast in October.

1989 Co-writer of *Fear and Misery in the Third Term*, ten short plays
on the effect of Thatcher's government in Britain; opened at
Liverpool Playhouse, spring, directed by Kate Rowlands and
opened at the Young Vic, London, in the autumn. Winner of
Time Out Theatre Award. *My Mother Said I Never Should*
broadcast on BBC Radio 4, 30 January, produced by Susan
Hogg. *My Mother Said I Never Should* opened at the Royal Court
Theatre, 23 February, directed by Michael Attenborough.
French première opened at the Gaite Montparnasse, Paris, 12
September, directed by Michel Fagadou. Swedish première
opened September. *Badger*, a children's television play,
televised on Granada TV, 26 June; nominated for a European
Prix Danube. *Is Green the Same for You*, a monologue about a

post-natally depressed woman, broadcast on BBC Radio 4 in the Young Playwrights' Festival in August. November: went to Berlin on Fall of Wall, and broadcast live piece on BBC Radio Cambridge Nine O'Clock News.

1989–90 Appointed Junior Judith E. Wilson Fellow in English at Cambridge University. Set up playwriting course for undergraduates.

1990 *Falling Slowly*, television film written for Channel Four and the European Co-Production Association commission. *My Mother Said* . . . premièred Holland, Singapore, Norway and USA. Translated into Czech.

1991 Writer-in-Residence for New York Stage and Film Company, May to July. Co-directed, with Dominic Cooke, world première of Heathcote Williams' *Autogeddon*, Assembly Rooms, Edinburgh Festival. Winner of a Fringe First.

1991–92 *The Singing Ringing Tree* opened at Contact Theatre, Manchester, 4 December, directed by Brigid Larmour. A musical play for children in the language of the old European folk tales. *My Mother Said* . . . premièred in Denmark, Finland, Australia and Germany.

1993 September: married in Crete. *My Mother Said* . . . premièred in Australia, Israel, Germany and Iceland; and designated a set text by UK examination boards for GCSE and A Level Theatre studies. Worked on new play *The Genius of Her Sex* about eighteenth-century mathematician Emilie du Chatelet.

1994 *Our Father* commissioned for Manchester City of Drama, about daughter-father relationships. *My Mother Said* . . . premièred in Italy, Spain, Norway and Greece.

1995–96 Adaptation of *The Tempest* with new scenes, performed by primary schools in inner city Manchester at Contact Theatre in April. *My Mother Said* . . . premièred in Prague and on Czech television.

1996 May: daughter Georgia born at home in Manchester.

1996– Ran workshops for British Council in India, Bosnia, and at
2000 University of Vienna; in the UK for Royal Court Theatre and Royal National Theatre, North West playwrights and many schools; and in Slovakia, Georgia and Shanghai – at the same time as bringing up her daughter as a single parent.

1997 April: marriage ends; divorce proceedings. Three-part dramatisation of Mrs Gaskell's *North and South* broadcast on BBC Radio 4, produced by Michael Fox, June–July. *My Mother Said...* major British tour and at the Young Vic, London, produced by Oxford Stage Company, directed by Dominic Cooke.

1999 *The Sleep of Reason Produces Monsters* premièred at Leeds Theatre Workshop and Shanghai Academy, China, co-directed with Mark Batty. *My Mother Said...* premièred in New Zealand, Poland, Ireland, and translated into Welsh, Georgian, Hebrew and Japanese.

1999– Twelve trips to the Republic of Georgia, working and
2006 travelling with filmmakers, shepherds, doctors, archaeologists, UN translators and Abkhaz and Chechens displaced by war.

2000 First draft of *Walking with the Travel Agents*, novel set in Georgia.

2000–5 *All the Daughters of War*, epic war play commissioned for the RSC, set in Georgia across 20 years.

2001 *Forest*, site-specific play for teenage performers at St Wilfred's School in Burnley, co-directed by Charlie Barrow.

2002 Researcher in Georgia, filming in children's prisons for documentary *Kids Behind Bars* produced by Brian Woods/True Vision, shown on Channel Four, winning an EMMY Award for the research team. Reading of *All the Daughters of War* directed by Michael Boyd with RSC in Newcastle.

2004–5 Wrote new draft of *All the Daughters of War* for RSC. *My Mother Said...* premièred in Japan.

2005 *The First Pirate Queen* premièred at Withington Girls School, Manchester, co-directed with Jenni Baylis. The play, for a cast of 50–70 young people, to be adapted for BBC Radio and published in 2006.

Foreword

Being asked to study a play on the page seems to me like being asked to read a cookery book and then describe how the meal tastes.

Once a play is written and published it is in the public domain. Anybody can stage it with whatever interpretation they choose. Ultimately it is the audience who decides if a production is authentic, and what the play means. This varies from one performance to another, according to the age and experience of the audience, the venue and even the weather.

The following sections describe my intentions at the time of writing the play; and my responses as I read the text now, examining it for clues about its meaning. Like anybody picking up this play, my response is subjective and personal. The best way to understand a play is to put it on its feet, even in a room.

Synopsis

Act One, Scene One: The Wasteground

Four little girls appear, singing the rhyme 'My Mother Said I Never Should'. Each child is dressed in the clothes of her childhood: Doris (1905), Margaret (1940), Jackie (1961) and Rosie (1979). Doris uses the accent and idiom of Oldham, Margaret of Manchester, Jackie and Rosie of south London. Yet they play together as if they are contemporaries. This is the first of five scenes in the 'wasteground', in a different time from the rest of the play.

Doris, the youngest at five, is taunted by the others to complete the rhyme 'What are little girls made of'. All of them cringe at 'Sugar and Spice', and Jackie suggests 'Let's kill our Mummy'. Jackie is the oldest, at nine, and appears to make decisions for the others. Margaret is also nine but seems younger. She wants Jackie to do things for her: she dares Jackie to kill their Mummy on their behalf, and is frightened of blood. Rosie is only eight but has a street-wise confidence, challenging Jackie and making her own observations: that they will become outlaws, or that the ghost of their Mummy might haunt them. Doris is shooed away, as the others think she will cry and Rosie says 'She'll split on us' (tell tales). Jackie starts some voodoo. Margaret announces she will never marry and therefore will never have babies; Rosie tells her there is a baby seed inside girls that can grow anyway. The three join hands and invoke the spirit of their Granny, to tell them how to kill their Mummy. Rosie and Margaret see something, scream and run off, abandoning Jackie. The ghost of a woman appears and starts walking towards Jackie, who calls for her Mummy and runs off after the others.

Act One, Scene Two: Cheadle Hulme, Christmas 1940/May 1961

The ghost walks downstage and as the lights rise, we see it is Doris, age 40. She pulls blackout material off a grand piano and dusts it lovingly, singing to a racy George Formby song on the radio. Margaret, eight, as in the child scene, surprises Doris from under the piano by shouting 'knickers'. She uses her doll Suky to suggest what Doris is thinking about; singing the nursery rhyme 'Suky take it off again' for its sexual innuendo. Doris pulls Margaret out and scolds her, threatening she will tell Margaret's father.

The room is austere and Doris is formal with her daughter, insisting on being called Mother not Mummy, and on piano practice, even though an air raid siren starts outside. They make up Margaret's bed under the piano. It is Christmas Eve but the room is without decoration except for a red bow around a vase of white wax roses. Margaret is spirited and full of questions; about bombs, Father Christmas, and whether her parents share a bed or say their prayers. Doris does not answer these, she responds with orders about Margaret's grammar or behaviour.

The air raid continues. Margaret is frightened but Doris will not offer comfort. Finally the little girl asks what happens when you die, to which Doris's reply is that she will bring Margaret some cocoa presently. Left alone, Margaret tells her doll that eight is too old for kisses.

The lights change to a spring morning, Doris is now 61 and granny to Jackie, the nine year-old we saw in the child scene. Jackie is visiting by herself, and is playing under the piano. Jackie asks why Margaret and Doris use the word Mother, whereas she uses Mummy; and she tries to understand how her Mummy has a Mother as well as being a mother herself. Doris is amused by all Jackie's questions, and answers them. Jackie has broken a utility mug from the war, Doris reassures her that she is still a very good girl. Doris suggests they make fairy cakes. Jackie hugs her Granny; Doris asks for a kiss, and they go off together.

The lights and sound return to the air raid for a moment as Doris re-enters with a utility mug of cocoa, but Margaret has fallen asleep in the dark.

Act One, Scene Three: The Wasteground

The characters reappear as children, as in Act One, Scene One. A scene of mystery and taboos. Rosie is waiting for Doris, to tell her that Mum has got the curse. Rosie uses the word 'curse' as slang for menstrual period, and thinks this might be the same sort of curse as in fairytales. She suggests to Doris that Mum's curse might be the result of their spell. Doris does not know about periods, only about fairytales. In their ignorance, the girls mix fairytale and common myth about periods; Doris asks if Mum pricked her finger and bled; Rosie announces that you have the curse until you are an old, old lady, then you die. They move into a game of doctors and nurses, in which they take turns to lie down while the other plays a male doctor examining a woman. Doris is scared of being touched between her legs, as her mother 'says she can see inside my head'. They repeat adult gossip as if this too is a kind of spell; Doris says her husband has upped and gone. They proceed to childbirth, which Doris says is like doing a big poo. Doris wants to play babies tomorrow but Rosie tells her that girls have to get married first.

Act One, Scene Four: Raynes Park, London, May 1969

Margaret aged 38, in an apron and clutching a tea towel, is trying to argue with her daughter, who has had first sex with her boyfriend. Jackie is 18 and sprawled on the grass in her flares, with her red transistor playing 'All You Need Is Love'. Margaret tries various maternal tactics including asking Jackie what she intends to tell her Daddy. Jackie replies that if Margaret wants her to behave like an adult, she should stop treating her like a child. She tells Margaret she has been on the Pill for a while. Margaret has been reading Jackie's diary, and Jackie confronts her mother with this. Margaret is flustered by Jackie's composure and speaks what she feels; that Jackie could have waited for sex until she was older, as she had had to herself. Jackie storms off. Margaret, left alone, picks up Jackie's transistor and recalls that she had an admirer who took her to dinner, but that was ten years ago.

Act One, Scene Five: Cheadle Hulme, Manchester, 1961

The garden becomes the lawn at the back of Doris and Jack's house, later on the same afternoon as Scene Two. Doris, 61, is arranging picnic tea on the lawn for Margaret's arrival. We hear

Jack mowing the lawn, he refuses to join them; but when Jackie runs out with Margaret, to show her the painting of the pear tree, Jackie says that Grandad let her use his real paints and showed her how to do shadows. Margaret has been away for the week with Ken, in the Lake District; she is 30, and it becomes apparent through the barbed comments of Doris (about taking iron tablets, and resting), that Margaret has suffered a miscarriage. Nine-year-old Jackie paints, within earshot.

Margaret, placed in a folding chair by Doris and balancing teacup and cake, is isolated and awkward. Doris and Jackie sit on the grass and remain affectionate. Jackie tells Margaret how she found Margaret's old doll, Suky, practised putting the doll to sleep and saw it close its eyes like a real baby. Margaret jumps up in distress; Jackie interprets this as Margaret thinking that Jackie has broken the doll. Doris understands otherwise and tries to hold Jackie, but Jackie is concerned only about her mother, and runs away, knocking the water pot across her precious painting. Doris picks this up, as evidence of the mess Margaret has made, and snaps that if Margaret hadn't been so hasty to get a temping (typing) job, she would never have lost the baby.

Act One, Scene Six: Hulme, Manchester, December 1971

A concrete council flat where Jackie, now 19, is trying to quieten her own tiny baby, Rosie, who has been yelling all night. Rosie, as an eight-year-old, is visible at the edge of the scene and makes the sounds of the baby but is not part of the scene. The red transistor from Act One, Scene Four, now battered, blares out the Rolling Stones. Jackie is packing baby clothes into carrier bags. Margaret walks through the open door, in her coat; Ken is waiting in the car; she has come to take the baby. The two mothers are nervous and uncertain of their feelings, offering comfort then anger in turns. The bags of baby clothes change hands each time they change their minds about who will take the baby.

Jackie says she made the agreement with Rosie's father, a married lecturer, that she would raise the child. But after three months alone, Jackie has phoned Margaret. Jackie says she will go back to art school, she won't fail both things. Margaret announces that Rosie will be told Jackie is her sister, and that Jackie can tell her the reality when Rosie is sixteen. Jackie is distraught and wants the bags back, but Margaret insists that Jackie has great opportunities. Jackie counters that these are Margaret's expectations of her; but relents. Margaret suggests Jackie stays with Doris and Jack until Christmas. She leaves Jackie one of the red socks which Rosie holds to go to sleep, and exits with the baby. Alone, Jackie empties the bag of Rosie's first baby clothes, and finally cries, first for Rosie, then for her own mother.

The lights go to black except for a spot in which we see Margaret cradling a bundle, comforting it first as Rosie, then as Jackie.

Act One, Scene Seven: Cheadle Hulme, Manchester, 1951

Margaret billows out the bundle as the lights come up on an August day in the garden: she is shaking out a white sheet. Doris takes the other end and they shake and fold, coming together and apart, as Margaret talks of her new life; today she leaves for London, and marriage with Ken, an American ex-pilot. Margaret announces she will do a typing course, and won't have children. Doris tells her that she too had a job once, teaching, and tells Margaret that she was ambivalent about having children, but Jack wanted a son. A thunderstorm is brewing and Ken's car horn announces his arrival; they must hurry with the washing on the line, and with this first and last conversation about love and marriage. Margaret runs off to greet Ken, leaving Doris alone. The rain starts, she half drops and half throws down the basket of worn linen.

Act One, Scene Eight: The Wasteground

The characters reappear as children, as in Act One, Scene One. Rosie is skipping alone, singing about boys: 'Georgie Porgie, Kiss the girls and make them cry'. Jackie runs in; she has been to the boys' den, a place some way off and dangerous for girls to go to. She went there bravely to retrieve her penknife from the boys, so that she and Rosie could make a vow, but had to give them bubble gum, and then a kiss. Rosie says this means they can't be best friends now. Jackie tries to make up, then cuts her finger and offers the blood to Rosie, who is impressed and does likewise. They make an honesty vow to remain best friends and Rosie adds that Jackie can never lie to her now. Rosie asks Jackie to look at the future for them, but Jackie warns against this with her mother's phrase, 'Don't cross bridges', which they repeat as a spell.

Act One, Scene Nine: Cheadle Hulme/Raynes Park, December 1971

Margaret has just arrived back in London with baby Rosie. It is the evening of the day in Scene Six when Margaret took Rosie from Manchester. Margaret is still in her coat as the telephone rings; it is her own mother, Doris, now 71, making their weekly call and commenting that Margaret usually phones before the six o'clock news. Flustered, and with Rosie's cries audible to Margaret in the background, Margaret is torn between the desire to tell her mother about the wonderful new baby, and the game of weekly small talk by which neither woman tells the other her true feelings. Doris asks why Jackie hasn't visited them for a year, despite living in Manchester now. They've not even had the usual hand-painted birthday card for Jack's birthday. Margaret fibs that Jackie is busy revising for her exams. Doris says Jack has now signed his will, and sold all his old easels, but wants Jackie to have his paint brushes. Margaret invites Doris and Jack to visit soon. Suspicious of this enthusiasm, Doris asks if this is to see the sofa Margaret had been planning to buy. Margaret falters and before she can explain, the habitual two minutes for their weekly call is up, and Doris puts the phone down.

Act One, Scene Ten: Raynes Park, September 1979

It is Rosie's birthday, but she storms into the garden intending to bury Suky. Rosie has attempted a punk haircut on the doll, which is now old, battered and naked, except for one red sock. Rosie is eight, the same age as Margaret in Scene Two, but Rosie is set on burying the doll because she feels she doesn't need dolls or her Mum any more. Rosie's interest is in Jackie. She tells Suky that no one else at school has a sister who's a grown-up, and that she might run away with Jackie and live with her. She digs a hole in the earth of a garden urn and pushes the doll into it. She resumes her painting, a picture of the cherry tree which she intends to give to Jackie.

Jackie enters with a shop-made cake, which Rosie finds odd; Margaret brings out drinks. They light candles but the two mothers conflict over how to make a wish and cut the cake; Rosie is upset. Jackie sees Rosie's painting, but Rosie, feeling confused by the conflict with Jackie, announces that the painting has gone wrong, and gives it to Margaret. Rosie runs into the house with the painting to stick it on the fridge.

Margaret says she's now working full time. Jackie is pleased and says she hopes to open her own gallery soon, with her ex-boyfriend Simon if she can raise the money. Margaret wishes Jackie would find a nice boyfriend, but Jackie replies that Simon wanted children, which only made her dream about Rosie. Jackie gives Margaret some lace made by Greek nuns, who Jackie says have used the same pattern for a thousand years. Then she offers a cheque towards the cost of raising Rosie, awkwardly explaining 'new bikes are expensive'. Margaret furiously tears up the cheque. Rosie, running out from the house, picks up the distress and tells Jackie she hates her, she then tugs Margaret to the kitchen to look at her painting. Alone, Jackie sees Suky sticking out of the urn, digs her out, takes the matching red sock from her pocket and puts it on the doll.

Act Two: Cheadle Hulme, December 1982

A cold room swathed in dustsheets, from which secrets emerge.

Rosie, now 11, enters the dark living room with a torch and addresses the ghost of Jack. Margaret is 51, she has driven Rosie and Doris, now 82, through the snow from London. Jackie, now 30, has brought a van from Manchester. Doris has been widowed a few months and the women have come to clear the house for sale. Jack has left the house and investments to Jackie in his will. Margaret and Doris take this as spite on Jack's part and resent Jackie for it. Doris observes that sixty years of housewifery have counted for nothing, in Jack's eyes, and refuses to choose items to take with her. Margaret who was born in this house also feels disinherited. Doris has decided to return to her roots, and has chosen an end-of-terrace cottage in Oldham which Jackie has bought for her. Rosie reminds them of this; she thinks the others are being unreasonable to Jackie.

Jackie organises the packing of crockery, ornaments and bedding. As they work, memories are raised by objects which we have seen in previous scenes, but the pain is often denied by the women. Rosie tells the older women they are being unfair to Jackie; Rosie is unintimidated by Jack's presence. She takes Doris off to the bedrooms where they cut up sheets to dress up as ghosts.

Alone together, Jackie sees Margaret is in pain; Margaret says this is just the menopause. Jackie offers to take Rosie in the holidays but Margaret rejects this offer. Jackie finds an old photograph which Margaret tells her is Doris's mother. Jack kept it hidden because Doris's mother was unmarried. Jackie is aghast that Margaret never told her that Doris was raised by her single mother. Rosie interrupts them, dressed as a ghost, and Jackie drops the photograph which smashes.

Rosie tells Jackie about arguments at home. Jackie is worried about everyone, she sees Jack's will as revenge, because she had escaped families, but is now responsible for everyone. Rosie suggests Jack did it so Jackie could open a gallery of her own. Rosie, saying that 'secrecy kills', makes a banner for an anti-nuclear demonstration out of the sheet, explaining that there are bigger things to worry about than what your mother thinks of you. She runs into the snowy garden waving the banner.

Doris enters. Fired up by Rosie's attitude to the house, she is throwing away old clothes, and the pale blue curtains chosen by Jack, declaring that she wants scarlet in her new house. Doris urges Jackie to ask for what she wants now, rather than resenting someone at the end of her life. Margaret enters and Jackie tries again to ask if she can take Rosie, but Margaret interrupts to ask her to sort out the spare room, and then exits again. Doris gives Jackie the baby clothes she has kept, which we saw Jackie holding at the end of Act One, Scene Six. Jackie cannot cope with this emotionally, so she goes to help Margaret. Doris calls Rosie from the garden to help her polish the piano. Rosie says she hates old things. Doris suggests 'You hate dead things, not old things, Rosie.

(*Pause.*) So do I. (*Pause*) I'm old.' She adds that if you are old and
angry people consider you senile. Rosie smooths away Doris's
wrinkles in an effort to show her that she is only old on the
surface. Their comradeship established, they polish the piano
together, and Doris even tells Rosie she had no father. Rosie asks if
this can be their secret. Rosie opens the bags of old clothes and
pulls out Jackie's hippy clothes (from Act One, Scene Six), and
Margaret's ski pants (from Act One, Scene Seven). Rosie puts on
the ski pants, disconcerting Doris – and Margaret, who enters
momentarily. Then Rosie finds her tiny baby clothes. Doris warns
her to put them back, but Jackie enters and sees. Before Jackie can
explain why they are here, Margaret enters and thinks Rosie has
been told about her real mother. The tension is diverted onto
everyone telling Rosie she is tired, and hurrying each other for
departure. Doris announces she is selling the piano, the only item
Jack left her in the will. Doris says it had belonged to her; she
bought it originally with her savings from teaching.

Doris is left alone while the others close up the house. In the
dark she tells Jack how the roses have all blown down in the
garden. She recalls nursing Jack and the day he died. Rosie re-
enters having found the solitaire board. Doris explains the game
belonged to her mother, and promises to show Rosie how to play
it, if Rosie visits her in Oldham. They take the solitaire board and
go out into the snow together.

Act Three, Scene One: Oldham, Backyard, April 1987

It is five years later and Doris, 87, has made a garden of tubs in the
backyard of her end-terraced cottage. Margaret, 56, has come to
visit, taking a day off work from her London office job. Rosie is on
holiday with Jackie for a week. The two women kneel together and
plant out geraniums, but Margaret is distracted; she tells her
mother that Ken has left her. Then Doris tells her daughter of the
distance in her own marriage, how Jack ceased to desire her, but
that one didn't divorce in those days. Margaret feels her marriage
failed because Ken wanted a wife, while Margaret has become a
working mother. Doris observes that each of them expected too
much; and that Jackie expects even more. Doris takes Margaret

indoors to show her the photograph of her mother, believing that Margaret has never seen her.

Act Three, Scene Two: Croydon, London, April 1987

Margaret is at her desk, early morning, when Rosie comes in with the office mail to surprise her. Rosie is now 15 and Jackie is 34, they have come direct from the airport, after their holiday. Rosie gives Margaret a blue kite from Venice, and enthuses about her week with Jackie, climaxing with the news that she wants to go and live with Jackie in Manchester, after her summer exams. Margaret is horrified but cannot tell Rosie about her real fear of losing her. She asks Rosie to leave her for a moment.

Jackie enters, smartly dressed for an important meeting about her art gallery, which she must attend today in Manchester. She is on her way to catch a train north, despite having been flying all night. Margaret is full of unspoken tension, which Jackie tries to unpick: she asks Margaret about her job, then her health. Jackie had arranged a appointment for Margaret to see a specialist about her pains, but Margaret brushes this aside as just menopause. For Jackie this relieves the tension; for Margaret this releases her anger and envy of Jackie's high-flying lifestyle and relationship with Rosie. Because Jackie has kept the promise of not yet telling Rosie who her real mother is, she enjoys a magical relationship with Rosie. Envious that Rosie has chosen Jackie, Margaret throws at Jackie the years of experiences she has lost; birthdays and snowmen and learning to ride a bicycle – and also reminds Jackie of the work she has put in looking after a child. Jackie is torn with guilt but Margaret insists Jackie must catch her train to Manchester; they both have work to do. When Jackie leaves, Margaret cries, realising she is a single woman again.

Act Three, Scene Three: The Wasteland

The characters reappear as children, as in Act One, Scene One. Rosie, Jackie and Doris are stirring a make-believe pot of spells together, casting a death wish on their mothers. Rosie and Doris become frightened of what it means to be dead, and want Jackie to undo the spell, but Jackie says they can't make someone's life go backwards. Doris and Rosie run off to find their mothers, leaving Jackie alone in the dark. She calls out that she didn't mean to make the curse, and doesn't want to be left alone.

Act Three, Scene Four: Hospital, Twickenham, London, May 1987

Margaret is in an operating gown. When she speaks we are hearing the voice in her head, as she is under anaesthetic. She is wandering backwards through her life, and has reached her childhood, in the austere house at Cheadle Hulme. She is trying to find the door to the garden. Instead she finds the bathroom, a cold hard place. She says father has made his fortune, but they must still make sacrifices, for piano tuition. Words stretch and drift, as she travels back into her childhood. As she nears death, reality mixes with fairytale images; the bath water roars down the plughole; her parents are called Guilt and Duty, her babies will be called Sugar and Spice. She repeats her line from Act One, Scene Two, where she asks her mother what happens when you die. The door opens, it's cold, Margaret keeps going towards the garden. We hear a child crying in the dark, then a baby.

Act Three, Scene Five: Raynes Park, London, May 1987

Rosie is in the garden, early morning, wrapped in a sweater of Ken's, listening to Jackie's red transistor – now very old and faded. Jackie rushes in, dressed smartly, having been up all night trying to get a plane back from Manchester, where she was due to open her new gallery. Rosie asks sarcastically whether Jackie's gallery was a success. Rosie tells her that Margaret died last night, and that Ken was with Margaret at the hospital. She died from stomach cancer. Jackie wishes she had been here with Rosie, and tells Rosie she cancelled the gallery opening in her effort to get back last night; Rosie refuses to believe she would make that choice. For once Jackie doesn't know what to do next. Rosie shows her Margaret's birth certificate, then her own. Rosie has discovered that Jackie is her real mother, five months before her sixteenth birthday, the age when Margaret would have allowed Jackie to tell Rosie herself. Jackie tells Rosie about her birth, her father who was married with two small children, and how she tried to manage alone. Rosie announces she is going to Oldham to live with Doris, and that she will never have any children.

Act Three, Scene Six: The Wasteground

The characters reappear as children, as in Act One, Scene One. Margaret as a child is tracing a line on the ground to play a boundary game, 'King Of The Golden River'. Jackie runs in and tries to cross the line to join her; Margaret catches her and asks her to do a dare. Jackie says she has; she went to the boys' den, and now the other girls won't play with her any more. Margaret offers to take Jackie to her secret hide, beyond the line, but Jackie chooses to go back. Margaret watches her go, then resumes her game, content to be alone as King.

Act Three, Scene Seven: Oldham, September 1987

Four months have passed. The backyard of Doris's end-terrace in Oldham, where Rosie now lives too. Rosie, dressed in home tie-dyed shorts and tee shirt, with her personal stereo on, is sitting in the sun playing with the solitaire board which is on the piano stool from Doris and Jack's house. Doris enters the backyard from the kitchen door, with a kite onto which she is sewing a tail.

Rosie now runs a small business printing logos on kites for charitable causes. Rosie persuades Doris to relax in the sun, and they discuss the painting which Jackie sent for Rosie's birthday this morning. Doris puts on some mirror sunglasses which she bought herself, and takes off her stockings so her legs can brown, something Jack would never have tolerated in a lady. They discuss the price of ice cream, the Queen Mother, the moors, Animal Liberation and Doris's evening class in Women's Literature, while Rosie tries to solve the solitaire. Doris gets up to make tea; she has got a birthday cake. Rosie tells Doris she loves her, Doris remarks that it's a long time since anyone said that to her. She gives Rosie the letter Jackie wrote to Rosie, to be opened on her sixteenth birthday, after Rosie was taken away by Margaret. Doris goes into the house. Rosie scans the letter, throws it down, then puts it in her pocket. She solves the solitaire, and calls Doris to show her.

There is no reply. Rosie sets out the marbles on the board to begin the game again.

Act Three, Scene Eight: Oldham, May 1923

Doris runs into the same space still occupied by Rosie from the previous scene. Doris is now twenty-three, dressed in the frock we saw Jackie pull from a bag at the end of Act Two, but here it is new. She is calling to her mother, in great excitement; Jack has proposed, although Doris cannot say so in those words. Doris describes the day out on the moors with Jack, taking the picnic her mother had made, and how she had to stare at the blue and yellow squares of the tablecloth while Jack proposed. Although enraptured, Doris hesitates to use the word 'love' to her silent Mother. Doris adds that she was promoted today, to Head of Infants, although Jack says she won't need to work after – again, Doris hesitates to use the word – 'marriage'. Doris has left Jack in the front room to ask Doris's mother's permission. Doris says she has seen the posy she wants, and concludes that she is so happy, this must be the beginning of her life.

Genesis

I wrote this play in 1985 when I was twenty-five. I had been making musical plays and performance art as an actor, director and designer for about four years. I had watched about 250 plays a year as a theatre critic – new and classic plays – in Britain and Europe. I had acted all sorts of parts, mostly waitresses, waifish daughters or disturbed children – the range of roles available to a small woman like myself. I had sat in dressing rooms thinking how there were a great many kinds of women who I had not seen in contemporary plays, so I decided I had better write the kind of play I would enjoy watching, or acting in.

I wrote it for four women because there are so few plays for women, compared to centuries worth of plays for men to act. It is traditional to see men onstage, like Hamlet, who are supposed to represent us all. In this play it is women who represent us all, and the massive social changes of the twentieth century. I wanted to show how hugely dramatic the 'ordinary' lives of women have been. The men are just offstage, as the women are in so many other plays.

It's hard to say how long it takes to write a play. I wrote this play in about three weeks, and spent three years re-writing it. For five years I had been living in Manchester and Leeds, listening to the way women talk, women whose lives were very different from my own. I was wondering what I would do with my life (I still am) and aware that I had many more choices than women in previous generations. I wanted to write a play which laid out four different lives, neither better nor worse, to find out what is possible for today. If I was writing this play now, I would do the same. I still don't know what kind of woman to be. I still don't have any children.

I split the century into four generations. I deliberately made Jackie and Rosie a little older and a little younger than me, because I didn't want to write from my own point of view. I connected the women as mother and daughter because I feel this relationship of love and jealousy most influences the choices a daughter makes. I also wanted to acknowledge the debt which my generation owes to previous ones. I made Jackie give away Rosie because I wanted to break the biggest taboo; a mother disowning her child.

Initially I wrote *My Mother Said I Never Should* fast and intuitively. Then I entered a process where I would stop and go over a piece of text, analysing, checking words, trying lines aloud, cutting whole scenes, adding new ones. This process continued through two readings and two productions, until I felt I had done my job. Every word in the finished text is there because it has been found useful in performance.

I felt as excited as being in love when I wrote the first draft. For a year the play was rejected by theatres, many of whom told me it was not a play because of its structure. Debbie Seymour directed a rehearsed reading with Paines Plough in London in March 1986. Ironically this fell on Mothering Sunday, so hardly anyone came. I also sent the play to Contact Theatre, Manchester. Brigid Larmour, then associate director, read it:

> When you showed me the first draft of *My Mother Said I Never Should* it immediately answered something inside me. I could absorb it into my blood as it were very quickly: the characters, structure and use of time.

We worked on the play through a reading at Northwest Playwrights' Workshop, and I listened to the audience's reactions. I re-wrote Act Two through the winter, typing in a sleeping bag because my cottage was so cold. Brigid used to bring me take-out curries and read through every line with me.

Brigid Larmour directed the première at Contact Theatre in February 1987. Rehearsing a new play is a process of negotiation. I had a strong sense of the vision of the play I was trying to make, which is vital, otherwise a playwright can be persuaded to change her or his play into one which the actors or director would rather produce. It was extremely important to me that the first production should be directed by a woman, because of the intuitive understanding Brigid and I shared, relating to the details of female experience which cannot necessarily be explained in words. Some of these are unconscious. Brigid Larmour:

> As director of a new play you have to do something slightly
> paranormal – you have to get into the head of the writer and
> understand what they intend. You have to develop and push that
> *before* you can query it, criticise or make cuts. Otherwise you're
> pulling the play off its centre. Then, once you understand the
> playwright's intention you can add your own vision.

The play was scheduled for nine performances, and shared a set
with two other productions, because of the financial risk of staging
new plays. We had to extend the run. I remember seeing people
queuing from the box office out into the street, and the following
day, hearing two women discuss the play in the doctor's surgery in
Gorton. They hadn't been to the theatre before.

Two years later the play was staged at the Royal Court Theatre,
London, in February 1989. Michael Attenborough, Director of the
Royal Court production:

> Second productions are, in my experience, important events in
> the lives of both plays and playwrights. Naturally the first
> production tends to be the most formative in terms of the text
> itself but a second allows the writer to return to the script with a
> greater degree of objectivity, benefiting also from the input of a
> director coming fresh to the play. Second productions in addition
> can rather crucially begin the process of allowing a writer to
> earn a living from that play, since only very rarely do they earn
> anything like the sum of money from the first production that
> would compensate them for the time spent in the writing
> process.

For this production I made some more changes to the text
including re-writing the whole of Act Two. Michael's observations
and criticisms helped me clarify the storytelling of the play.

In this second production I learned how the play text could be
directed by a man. I think that by the time the playwright has
worked over the text, and through a first production, the play is
like a map. I have made this play as accurate and detailed as
possible so that anyone can take it and find its territory. Michael
chose to cut the last child scene, whereas Charles Towers, in a
Boston, USA production, found it essential. Directors will make
decisions based on their personality and gender. The female
unconscious and magic of this play will appear in performance
because it is in the play, whether or not it is in the director.

The Languages of Playwriting

The word playwright has the same ending as shipwright, wheelwright and cartwright: a maker of vehicles in which other people can make journeys. I began *My Mother Said I Never Should* with the structure and built it in three dimensions in my head before applying words. I started writing in the languages of light, colour, environment, sound, object, costume and action or dance. The playscript on the page is a temporary stage between the writer's imagination and the public performance. After I had 'written' much of the play in these terms, the role of the dialogue was clear. The words don't have to establish situation and meaning, so they can play against these, as explained in the section on Language. The theatrical languages below are explained in the order I used them to write the play.

Icon images: the beginning and end of scenes

I started making scenes by thinking of the *image* which would sum up the scene. Margaret standing holding a tea towel while Jackie sprawls face down on the grass in her hippy clothes, with her transistor blaring 'All You Need Is Love', tells the audience what is at stake in this scene, as well as the time, place and status of the characters. Every scene in the play starts with a particular image like this, and ends with a contrasting one. There are also some key images during the scenes, for example in Act Two where Doris is sitting looking at her face in the salver while Rosie smooths away her wrinkles (p. 58).

I think we remember the images of a play long after we have forgotten the words, so I began this play by trying to find the image for each scene which would sum up its meaning. I also feel that theatre works most effectively at this unconscious level, rather like dreams, where one image holds several meanings simultaneously, some of which can never be explained in words.

The end-images of scenes are more surreal, or non-naturalistic.

For example Doris dropping the basket of washing as the thunder breaks at the end of Act One, Scene Seven. These end-images are intended to float beyond the time of the scene, like images from the unconscious of the woman who stands there. For example, Jackie cradling a bundle of Rosie's clothes at the end of Act One, Scene Six, changes to an image of Margaret cradling a white bundle, and comforting it as a baby who is both Rosie and Jackie. This then becomes Margaret shaking out a sheet she is folding on a summer's day, before she is even married.

In performance terms, these images need to be choreographed as carefully as the words are rehearsed. They indicate that the play is not entirely naturalistic. I didn't think about styles at the time, but I suppose the play is expressionistic in its selective and heightened use of reality. This signals to the designer that if set design is cluttered, the images won't have the same impact. In my mind's eye the images glow against the dark in colour and shape, like icons of women's lives across the century.

The images are not described by stage directions, but by dialogue which leads characters into certain gestures or actions. In the process of rehearsal such images are discovered. This process is linked to the section on dance and is best explored through practical work (see Appendix: Exercise 11).

Light

Light rather than set is specified for transforming the stage space from one time and place to another. The light is naturalistic – a summer storm, a spring dawn, light reflected off snow, encroaching night. The idea is that the audience and actors will recognise and identify with the experience of being in the real place. But light is used as much for its psychological effect. An August afternoon with thunder rumbling evokes an imminent argument and sudden change (Act One, Scene Seven). A spring dawn evokes a vulnerable new beginning (Act Three, Scene Five). The kind of light chosen for each scene in the play affects behaviour, even the way characters talk. I use light to set up the potential of a scene. Imagine how different Act One, Scene Two would be if Margaret and Doris were in a sunny room instead of midwinter in the blackout (see Appendix: Exercise 6).

Colour

Colour functions non-naturalistically in the play. Certain colours predominate; scarlet, white and silver. Scarlet is the colour of blood and passion; it appears in intense splashes – geraniums, socks, drops of blood, the transistor radio, one ribbon in a dark room, Doris's curtains. White appears in swathes; snow, sheets, dustsheets, frozen roses, an operating gown – deadening or masking emotion, waiting for something to happen. Green, blue and orange are specified only once, as kites given to characters at a moment of particular spiritual significance. Exploring colour language through workshops in schools, I have found we all share a universal understanding of colour, which crosses language barriers (see Appendix: Exercise 7).

I did not plan the use of colours consciously, as I did with light. Thinking in sensual terms my mind selected a colour code without realising it – just as we choose a certain colour to wear for a certain occasion. The designer of the Birmingham Repertory Theatre production in 1992 used Freud's book on dreams to analyse all the colours and images in the play and she told me they are all female archetypes. It seems to me that theatre is capable of speaking directly in the language of our unconscious. When I was writing a children's musical, *The Singing, Ringing Tree* in 1991, based on European folk tales, it struck me that the colours in *My Mother Said I Never Should* are those which predominate in folk tales; red blood, white snow. They give a sense of magic powers at work in characters' lives in the way they recur at particular moments in a story.

Environment: no sofas in this play

'There are no sofas in this play. The set should be a magic place where things can happen.' Charlotte Keatley (see cast list page 3).

I use the word environment rather than 'set', because I want the best space in which a scene can happen, and not a set to enclose it. I wrote this play to explore the behaviour and communication of people, so I want there to be as little as possible to distract us from watching the actors.

A teacher asked me recently why I specified no sofas, when Doris

seems a particularly sofa kind of person. This identifies exactly
why there are no sofas, or chairs – only three folding garden chairs
– in the whole play. If Doris or any of the characters could sit
down, they could be comfortable. I wanted the women to appear
awkward or uncomfortable, because this is what is happening
emotionally and psychologically. The majority of scenes take place
in gardens, because people are more exposed physically and
emotionally when outdoors. There is no furniture to hide behind so
the action has more dramatic impact. Outdoors is also a
potentially freer space for women than that of domestic rooms, so
there is more possibility for change.

Environment is as much a signal to the actor as the designer.
One of the first decisions I made about the play was that there
would be *no kitchen scenes*; the predictable setting for a play about
mothers and daughters. The environment of a scene is chosen to
heighten dramatic tension. Unexpected places reveal more;
Christmas during an air raid, a child's swing for a bereavement;
children in a dark patch of wasteground beyond the reach of
adults. I deliberately set the crisis moments of female choice – child
versus career – in the most male-created environments: Jack's
house, Jackie's council-flat and Margaret's office. The environment
makes it harder for the women to say what they want and feel; and
it actually represents the masculine side of the emotional choice
that Margaret and Jackie are trying to make. A line which
demonstrates how environment works with character and theme, is
in the office in Act Three:

Margaret (*pause. Pleased*). It's funny, hearing 'Mummy' in this
    place. (p. 76)

Dramatic dynamic comes from the contrast of settings; we move
from dark wasteground to suburban garden, cold concrete flat to
hot August lawn, backyard to office. The floor is the key to the
design. However, the basic floor and backdrop cannot belong to
one particular time and place, or the other scenes will appear to be
flashbacks. The design carries the meaning of the play as much as
any other medium.

Earth is the base element of the play. I think the stage floor is the
key to the design – grass, a worn rug, a stone backyard. It is only
when the characters touch earth that they make contact with their

true feelings and powers. All the child scenes take place on bare earth. On her birthday, Rosie buries Margaret's doll in the soil. When Doris and Margaret finally kneel together with their hands in the soil, planting geranium seedlings, they speak their real feelings. Margaret, as she dies, is trying to find the garden. There are key moments of contact with the earth throughout the play.

In three different productions of the play, in Britain, Germany and America, the actor playing Jackie has kicked off her shoes before her long speech to Rosie in the garden in Act Three, and chosen to stand in bare feet – instinctively enacting the metaphor of earthing herself. This is not specified as a stage direction; it happens spontaneously in performance because the environment provides the actor with the means to express the scene. In this way, environment can announce the drama of a scene with more power and theatricality than words (see Appendix: Exercise 8).

Dialogue is determined by environment. If four people arrive at the snow-bound house of a dead man, without much time to pack up a cold room, where objects are hidden under sheets and there are no comfy chairs, then their dialogue will be agitated. The environment creates the dramatic tension of grief, fear of dying and an uncertain future. The dialogue can then work in contrast to the visual setting. I wanted to create a sensory experience for the audience, for the audience to feel the play in their bodies as much as in their heads.

Sound

Sound has two roles in the play. The first is naturalistic and I planned these carefully; every scene begins with a sound cue which locates time and place. Sound also defines size and distance in the environment; the wasteground is beyond all sound except that of cats wailing. Traffic noise outside Margaret's office, and the blaring radio inside Jackie's flat add to the oppressive lack of personal space.

The second function of sound I only noticed when I was analysing the text recently with a school group in Manchester. The sounds in the play: lawnmower, traffic, an icecream van, Ken's car horn, two male radio announcements and four male popular songs, are mostly mechanical, and seem to me to represent the offstage world of the men. The sounds come right up to the edge of the space the women make for themselves – and sometimes break into it. So, while there are no men 'in' the play, there are men all around it. There are only two organic sounds in the play; cats wailing in the wasteground, and babies crying. They evoke female magic.

Objects

The objects written into the play are very ordinary ones, which take on extraordinary powers because of the way they appear, and reappear. I think the use of objects enacts the conventions and themes of the play more clearly than any other aspect of staging.

The symbolism comes out of the use of the objects, not the other way round. No object should be onstage unless it is used for a real purpose. In this way, an object becomes symbolic by being part of an emotional event; as in Jackie keeping one of her baby's red socks when she gives Rosie away to Margaret. Whenever the object reappears, such as Jackie taking the red sock from her pocket at the end of Act One, it brings that emotional history onstage. This may be acknowledged, as with the solitaire board in Act Three, Scene Seven. More often it is ignored, as with the utility mug in Act Two (p. 48), at which point the objects become dangerous, taboo items – as dangerous as a knife appearing onstage. The objects in the play are the weapons of the female rites of passage.

As with environment, I start by thinking about the actor. What objects does Doris need, to show the austerity of Margaret's upbringing, in Act One, Scene Two? What objects do Doris and Rosie need to show us their inventive lifestyle in Act Three, Scene Seven? Our minds select objects when we want to remember a particular event. They also remind us that there are always several versions of one story. In Act Two the baby clothes elicit three different versions of the past from three different perspectives: Rosie's, Jackie's and Margaret's. Objects are part of the myth-making in the play (see Appendix: Exercise 9).

The set design needs to focus our awareness of the objects. A production of the play at the West Yorkshire Playhouse in 1991 consisted of a mountain of objects from four generations, which dominated the stage and onto which the actors climbed. I felt this announced that the play was about the past, rather than a series of present day scenes, and that the individual power of objects was lost against the vast heap. At Chichester Festival Theatre in 1990, the set was non-naturalistic and the piano was a crate of rough planks, which later became Margaret's office desk. The solid presence of the piano, with the smooth dark wood which is touched and polished in different scenes, was lost. The element of make-believe was heightened. In a play which sets *real* objects in *unreal* time, the designer needs to draw a clear line between these. I have also chosen objects for their colour, texture, shape and the way they reflect light.

Costume

All clothes are a costume through which we announce a character. Some costumes are written into the play because they represent the energy or behaviour of a person. The reappearance of *old* clothes brings onstage a sense of a character's past behaviour. Worn by a different woman in the present, the costume creates dramatic irony. Costumes are also part of the myth-making of the play; the ski-pants in Act Two suggest different past versions of Margaret to herself, Doris and Rosie, in the present.

Women's fashion changes every half decade or so, therefore costume is a useful device to locate the time of a scene. However, I was most interested in how costume is integral to the theme of expectations: society's notion of feminine behaviour is reflected in the shape and fabric of women's clothes. Children's clothes dictate a type of girl. This is useful to the actor, because the costumes describe a body shape and way of moving which helps the actor radically change her attitude, as well as age and appearance from scene to scene (see Appendix: Exercise 10).

Certain costumes are written into the play because these are necessary for the meaning of a scene. The ski-pants, for example, evoke sex, America, the fifties or mid-eighties, masculine energy and a desire to be modern – contrasted with Doris's beige skirt. All the costumes specified in the stage directions are part of the symbolic language of the play. Other costumes are decided by the costume designer, according to the style of the production.

The dance

Each scene has a dance running through it, which is the physical manifestation of the meaning of the scene. By dance, I mean the patterns of movement and activity as well as the distances between the performers in the space. The so-called dance acts out the subtext of each scene. In the adult scenes, the dance expresses the violence or anger which the words tiptoe around. In the child scenes, the dance is a grotesque version of the adult dance, pushed to its limit. The audience may laugh at the mimicry, as when Rosie and Doris explore sex in Act One, Scene Three, but they are exploring the dance of rape and then the dance of a woman giving control of her body to a man (see Appendix: Exercise 11). Dance gives us direct access to taboos and rituals in a society.

The status and intention of each woman is announced by how she is standing, sitting or lying at the beginning of each scene. No two women sit together until the penultimate scene of the play. The distance of one woman from another announces their relationship. They move forward and back, sometimes able to touch, often not. Compare the two kinds of dance between a woman and child in Act One, Scene Two.

Once I had worked out the dance, I could write the dialogue. With Jackie lying on her front in Act One, Scene Three, Margaret is clearly not going to win the argument. In Act One, Scene Seven, the dance of Doris and Margaret folding sheets, together and apart, sets in motion their argument of conflicting and connecting desires. The dance of each scene is not described by stage directions but by a dialogue which clearly requires action to make sense.

Production photographs included in this edition display some of the dance of the play.

Commentary

Use of Time

Stage time

It is most important in the staging of this play that no time is presented as the past, otherwise the play becomes nostalgic or sentimental. The reason I specify that the set should be 'a magic place where things can happen' is that by staging all times on the same spot we enact the idea in the play that all past time is present inside us.

The child scenes give all four women the chance to escape time altogether; there is no envy, there is no perception of one person being mother to another either further back or forward in time. I wanted to explore how mothers and daughters could share common experiences if not divided by time and age.

We have centuries of plays in which men dominate the stage time, while women characters appear as noble supportive wives, mothers or girlfriends. Shakespeare's *Julius Caesar*, *Coriolanus* and *Macbeth*, Arthur Miller's *Death of a Salesman* and contemporary plays such as David Hare's *Racing Demon* demonstrate this. The convention partly exists because, until the late 1960s, so few women wrote plays. In *My Mother Said I Never Should* I wanted to show what those wives, mothers and girlfriends were doing in all that offstage time.

Women may appear as supportive and selfless, but I don't believe women are 'better' or more virtuous than men, and it is unfair for women to have only this role in plays. I see my play as a violent one, and the way that women show violence as being through words, subtext and silences, rather than fists or swords.

The cost of maintaining the role of the good woman, is often resentment and suppressed anger. After a sixty-one-year marriage, Doris warns Jackie:

Doris I never did ask for what I wanted . . . You don't want to be resenting somebody at the end of your life. (p. 55)

I wanted to dramatise the emotional inheritance of women's lives. 'Withering puritanism', Michael Billington called it: 'this vision of life as an endless cycle of sacrifice and struggle' (*Guardian*, 1989). Suppressed resentment is carried on to the next generation, and the next – because women like Doris don't feel they can get angry, or ask their husbands to change, and share the time load of raising a family. Margaret continues the tradition; it is she not Ken who raises Rosie, and tries to shoulder a job as well:

Rosie She's doing some new computer course in the evenings.

Jackie Does Dad mind?

Rosie Yeah, Mum drives him spare. They have rows a lot.

Jackie (*anxious*) What about?

Rosie Oh, I dunno, the washing or something. I just put my Walkman on. (p. 53)

Even Jackie, in the above example, sounds more concerned about her father's evenings than her mother's. As a desperate single mother, Jackie never asked Graham, the married father of Rosie, for help. When she finally sought him out he had moved house without telling her. After the American première, I had some furious men attack me for Jackie's selfishness in giving her child away to pursue her own career. 'That's why modern marriages don't work, because women want careers!' one said to me. I asked him why he wasn't angry with Graham for totally abandoning Rosie and then moving out of contact for the rest of her life.

Female use of time

I believe that the women who have written a substantial amount of the significant British plays of the last twenty-five years, have developed a 'female aesthetic' in theatre writing. The plays of Caryl Churchill, Sarah Daniels, Anne Devlin, Liz Lochead, Sharman MacDonald and Sheila Yeger are very different, but I think that many of their plays experiment with structure and use of time, to a much greater degree than those of our male contemporaries. I did not see Caryl Churchill's *Top Girls* or Sharman MacDonald's *When I Was A Girl I Used To Scream And Shout* until after I had written *My Mother Said I Never Should*. So I find it even more exciting and intriguing that, in order to dramatise women's experiences, we all experiment with non-linear time.

I began to question why this might be. I think most women are taught a different emotional idea of time from men. Firstly, time is always running out for women; there is always too much to do, women seem to spend so much time looking after other people – often at the expense of themselves. Secondly, a woman's internal clock is ticking throughout her life until she can no longer bear a child. A woman may be able to make time her own before she has a child, but afterwards, time will never be entirely her own. So I think the way I use time to structure the play – juxtaposing different times to create urgency and dramatic tension – comes from my own experience of time in everyday life. This is why I don't feel that reading Brecht or Stanislavski would help me make plays; I am trying to convert a different life experience into theatre, so I must make my own conventions.

My use of time, with past episodes being brought up into the present, is devised to show how the emotional inheritance of women is handed down, and how this affects present and future possibilities.

Whether or not we have children, I think most women are taught very early on that our time is not for us; it is to be used for doing things for other people. So in the play the women are always working while they are talking: folding washing, packing up a house, planting seedlings or polishing a piano; even Rosie, in the penultimate scene, is making kites for a charitable cause – not for herself. When I see plays by men, I notice how rarely they are actually working while talking. I wanted to show women's lives as I see them, not a theatrical version.

The myth about women is that they sit and gossip, but my experience is that we rarely use time just to discuss our lives, even at incredibly important emotional moments. Women are the losers; Margaret asks teenage Jackie why she went on the (contraceptive) pill and slept with her boyfriend without discussing it:

Jackie Well I did say I wanted to have a talk with you, actually, and you said 'Tell me while we go round the garden centre', don't you remember? (p. 19)

Jackie and Margaret have their final and devastating confrontation over who will take Rosie, in Margaret's office. It is early morning, and Margaret is trying to sort her post, while Jackie, who has been flying all night, has to catch a train to a key meeting in Manchester about her art gallery.

Margaret Are you going to catch that train, or stay here? You can't do both. (p. 78)

When Jackie rushes out of the office, Margaret bursts into tears. The boss phones at this moment, but Margaret merely says 'I'll be with you directly,' (p. 78) wiping tears and mascara off the morning post.

So, not only are the women in the play always working, but the time they do have alone is often cut short by the arrival of a man. He would probably never realise what the women were talking about or dealing with, as the women keep this quiet. I wanted to show how hard it is for women to ask for time for their own needs. On the day Margaret is to leave home forever, she has a rushed conversation with Doris about babies, careers, marriage, and sexual desire, in between folding sheets and taking Jack's socks and shirts off the line, and before getting tea ready for Ken – whose car horn interrupts them.

I think this denial of personal time is why it has been so hard, for centuries, for women to become artists; art is felt to be selfish in a woman because it's about self-expression. I think this internal dilemma is an even bigger pressure than the practical constraints that have held women back.

In this respect, Jackie is a double first in her family; the first woman who holds onto her time to make a career is also an artist. Her work has glamour, and idealism. We might expect the older women in the family to be proud – as Jack is. Their opinions come out when the women clear Jack's house – Act Two is continual orchestrated cleaning and tidying – and we learn that he has left everything to Jackie in his will:

Doris It seems that sixty years of housewifery counted for nothing, in Jack's eyes.

Margaret Your house has always been a gleaming example to us, Mother. Rosie, can you fetch some more newspaper please.

Doris Well Jackie didn't follow it, did she. (*Slight pause.*) Jack noticed *her* sort of work, because he was always asking how her painting exhibitions were going. And since Jackie didn't care to visit much, I had to make it up. And as you know, modern art was never my strong point.

Rosie She hardly ever visits us, Gran.

Jackie – I'm always there for your birthdays, Rosie.

Rosie Most of them.

Jackie I try.

Rosie S'okay Jackie, you have to travel lots, and your work's the most important thing, isn't it. (*Pause.*)

Margaret Funny how a job was never a good enough excuse for me. I think Father disapproved of it. (pp. 47–8)

Margaret and Doris find Jackie's use of her time unacceptably selfish. Yet it was Margaret who goaded Jackie to give her Rosie and take up a career in art. Women can be more critical of another woman trying to break the mould, than they would ever be of a man who makes mistakes. I wanted to show this. The play is not simply a criticism of male culture, but an exposure of women's responses. Envy can hold women back as much as self-sacrifice. Annie Castledine, who directed the 1990 Chichester Festival production, observed:

> This is a frightening play, because it shows women as they really are to one another, which is very different from how they behave to men.

How did Jackie manage to succeed as an artist? By giving up her motherhood and with it, her female attitude to time. Jack hardly seems to think of her as a woman. It was long after writing the play that I noticed I had given Jackie a version of her grandfather's name. But I was aware that Jackie chooses the career Jack had once dreamed of following. From childhood, painting with Jack's paints, Jackie follows the male line, not the female, in her use of time. Years later, she realises the deal:

> **Jackie** You know Mummy, the gallery and everything, I couldn't have done it without you. You can't be a mother and then cancel Christmas to be in New York. (p. 78)

It is almost as if Jackie has been the absent but successful *husband* to Margaret who stayed at home and raised the child. She tries to compensate as breadwinner; in Act One, Scene Ten, Jackie brings a birthday cake for Rosie (bought not made), and a cheque and lace for Margaret; in Act Three, Scene Two, she has taken Rosie on holiday and paid for Margaret's health care. The agony for Jackie is that, playing both woman and man, she experiences the guilt and loss both of absent mother and absent father:

> **Jackie** We were running along this dazzling beach. I thought, is this what I've missed?
>
> **Margaret** Years and years and years you've lost, Jackie. Birthdays and first snowman and learning to ride a bicycle and new front teeth. You can't pull them back.
>
> **Jackie** I can make up for it – somehow –
>
> **Margaret** You can't. Those are my years.
>
> **Jackie** She must remember – I visited!
>
> **Margaret** Treats, she's had with you. A day here and there. That never fooled her. But I let it fool you. I'm the woman who sat up all night with the sick child, who didn't mind all her best crockery getting broken over the years.
>
> **Jackie** Mummy . . .
>
> **Margaret** (*long pause. Cool*) What time's your train?
>
> **Jackie** 9.45 – no – I could get the 10.45.
>
> **Margaret** You mustn't miss your meeting.
>
> **Jackie** It would give us another hour. I wish we weren't in your office! (*Panics.*) Where's Rosie gone?

Margaret Are you going to catch that train, or stay here? You can't do both. (pp. 77–8)

When dividing the play, I consciously split the century into the four ages which I felt marked the greatest, most dramatic changes in women's lives. Doris gave all her time to family: 'There wasn't any choice, then.' (p. 31) Both Margaret and Jackie's generation try to juggle time between work and home. Margaret gives the greater share to home, and although exhausted and finally ill, she wears the mantle of virtuous suffering which women have worn on stage and in life for centuries – though it may hide daggers of resentment. Jackie shifts the balance of her time towards her own life and career. Jackie breaks the chain of emotional inheritance, because Rosie is not brought up by a resentful mother. Margaret is a grandmother who has chosen to take on a child; there is still resentment, but this is directed at her daughter, Jackie. Rosie escapes. I have heard Jackie criticised for her 'selfishness' at giving up her child, but rarely credited for what she shoulders in order to set Rosie free.

The final irony for Jackie is that on the day she cancels work – the opening of her own gallery, at last – to be with Rosie and Margaret, she loses them both. Rejecting Jackie as her mother, Rosie literally throws back at Jackie all the pieces of time they had together; the photographs of birthdays and holidays over the years (p. 83).

When I hear people dismiss the word feminism as an embarrassing over-reaction by women in the seventies and eighties, it seems to me we are ignoring the stress carried by women like Jackie. It's easy for Rosie's generation to take their freedom for granted and simply see Jackie as indecisive. When Rosie makes a banner protesting at nuclear secrecy, Jackie makes one saying 'Sorry Mummy':

Rosie You should stop that sort of thing now, or you never will. You should hear Mum's 'I'm sorry' voice on the phone to Gran. (p. 54)

For Rosie the choice is clear; your life is your own.

This is the major reason for inventing the plot of Jackie giving Rosie away; I wanted to explore what would happen if women are not raised by their mothers, in that cradle of love and envy. In the penultimate scene, Rosie is able to say to Doris, who is about to tidy her room:

> **Rosie** It's not for you to clear up. Sit down Doris, enjoy the sun. (p. 86)

The triumph is that Rosie does not feel guilty either; she does not rush off to tidy the mess herself. So at the end of the play we do actually see two women stop working, sit down – relaxed – and simply enjoy each other's company (Act Three, Scene Seven). I wanted to give a basking, contented possibility at the conclusion of this play, even though I can't write a 'happy ending' in the sense of an answer to the mother-daughter relationship.

The dilemma of time for women is summed up for me by the decision of a British woman director to *cut* some of the dialogue of this penultimate scene, because she felt it was too long for women to be just sitting talking together.

Structure

In his review of the 1989 Royal Court production for the *Telegraph*, Charles Spencer wrote:

> Instead of presenting a straightforward narrative, she chops her story up into gobbets and arranges them with no regard for chronology.

Theatre critic, Lyn Gardner, saw the play at the same time and wrote:

> This is a landmark play. The theatrical equivalent of breaking the four minute mile; like Caryl Churchill's 'Top Girls', pointing the way for the next generation of playwrights in form and content.

I began writing the play by inventing the structure of non-chronological time, spliced with five scenes where the characters meet in a place outside all chronology. I had to begin with the structure, because for me it explains the intention of the play.

By structure I mean *how* the story is told; the order of scenes, the length of scenes, of acts, and of the play. This includes who we see first and last, where the monologues come, where there is silence, or a key image. Structure fascinates me; the decisions about what to show onstage, and what to leave out, are what makes my play distinct from the way someone else might tell the same story. In this way, I feel that the structure tells the audience what a play means, far more than the dialogue within the structure, which is where we often look for meaning.

The meaning of the structure

If I wrote the story of the four women and their family in chronological order then it would be a history play. I jumble time and childhood because this is not a play about the past, but about how the past continually interrupts the present and informs our present-day decisions. I wanted to write a play which questions why certain life-changing decisions are made, rather than simply showing what happens in the story of four lives.

We read order of sequence to be order of importance. The order and amount of time given to one character or another suggests who is most important in a play, and who it belongs to. Stage time in *My Mother Said I Never Should* is structured to belong equally to four characters. When I was writing the play, I visualised it as a dance for four women.

The structure gives a play meaning even before a character speaks. The first image of the play is four girls who enter together. By showing the characters first as children, we see their potential to be equals, before they are separated, with different status, into generations of mother and daughter. If I started the play with Act One, Scene Two, the play would first belong to Doris; our first impressions of Margaret or Jackie would be that they are children, and we would not even know that Rosie existed.

The first scene also announces the conventions of this play to an audience; that actors will be playing ages very far from their own age; and that different times and generations may be put onstage simultaneously.

Act One: Emotional chronology

The structure of Act One dramatises the process by which we learn about the past. It is about how the past is continually alive inside us, and can be called up at any moment.

Having invented a family, I structured Act One so that the audience learns about the four generations in the jigsaw puzzle way pieces of a family's past are given to a child. As we grow up, we are fed bits of emotional or factual information, in the order our families think it is most important for us to learn about them. In family life we don't learn about the past in a chronological order, although at school we are taught history in this order. And we don't usually store memory in chronological order either, but in an order I call *emotional chronology*; the most important events in our past are usually the ones we remember first (see Appendix: Exercise 5).

Act One also dramatises how we move from one time to another effortlessly inside our heads, every day. While you are reading this page, you may be reminded of some event from childhood, which might remind you of something a friend said to you yesterday. It takes only seconds to pass between these three time scenes, and they all exist within you in the present.

The child scenes also function like this. Each one is clearly related to the subject of the scene before and after it. The child scenes are the deepest memory but are just as much part of the present story.

Act Two: The past

Act Two shows how the past is continually surfacing in the present. Fifty years of history is stored in the objects and clothes in one room, and these trigger unresolved memories as the women move about trying to clear up the past. Act Two shows how each woman decides to accept or deny this emotional inheritance.

Rosie is not intimidated by the past; she explores the bedrooms, tips out bags of clothes, and asks about objects. She stirs up Doris to question her past with Jack and the values that he represents. Rosie seizes the emblem of Jack's career:

Rosie (*sniffs*) The silver smells funny. I hate old things.

Doris You hate dead things, not old things, Rosie. (*Pause.*) So do I. (*Pause.*) I'm old. (p. 57)

For me, this is the structural pivot of the play. The most weary cynicism about the future, in Doris, meets the most buoyant rejection of the past, in Rosie. Doris stops dying and starts a new life with a vengeance which re-vitalises the play.

Margaret and Jackie cannot confront their past in Act Two as they are too frightened to look at what they have done, or not done:

Rosie *passes mug to* **Jackie**, *who wraps it.*

Jackie Oh yes – I broke the handle once – see where Grandad glued it?

Margaret I don't remember.

Jackie Oh – you weren't here.

Margaret Why ever not?

Jackie Well it was the summer you – (*Stuck.*) – weren't well.

Margaret (*pause*) I don't remember. (p. 48)

Here Jackie reminds her mother of the summer Margaret had a miscarriage, but Margaret chooses not to remember. The crisis point of their denial of the past is the appearance of the baby clothes. Because Margaret and Jackie try to deny whose they are, this past moment becomes a time bomb ticking through Act Three.

Act Three: The future

Act Three shows the result of the women's decisions in Act Two. Rosie and Doris have accepted what happened, even their losses. They literally leave behind the objects and clothes except for the solitaire board belonging to Doris's mother. In Act Three they are free to invent new lives for themselves. The curve of their lives rises, Rosie's continuing beyond the end of the play.

There is a tragic curve downwards through Act Three, in the other two lives. Jackie and Margaret are still using their energy to cover over the past, so they are unable to make a new start. Both of them lose their daughter, Rosie, which, in a way, is like losing their relationship to the future. Margaret carries so much unresolved grief that she loses her life. This final shock to Jackie – who loses both her mother and daughter – finally enables her to leave the past. In the penultimate scene we hear she is making a new life in Manchester. Margaret is last seen as a child waiting her turn for the new game to begin. (Act Three, Scene Six) The child scenes complete a cycle that is not an end.

There is one more surprise in the structure; as it reaches the end of the adults' story, the structure brings us to the beginning. Doris's engagement speech is the first moment a woman speaks of her *future*. By setting it against the final outcome of her life and those of three subsequent generations, the structure places an ironic question about expectations at the end of the play, and is in counterpoint to the image of Rosie sitting at the solitaire board ready to go out into the world.

Structure and pace

The rhythms and pace of the play are created by the structure, not the plot. I think of playwriting as close to music, and three acts, like three movements in a symphony, provide three overall approaches to the same themes. Act One is a jigsaw puzzle of time and information, the pace coming from the juxtaposition of different times and places. Act Two offers a calmer unity of continuous time, and it is deliberately the only place where all four women consciously meet. The energy comes out of the clash of attitudes of the four generations. There is a complicated internal structure of tiny scenes in Act Two, woven out of the four voices moving in and out of the room and sometimes coming together to create a crescendo.

Act Three covers a much shorter time period than Act One – six months instead of fifty years. Accelerated time creates a sense of urgency. The last two child scenes appear in this Act, bringing to a conclusion the story being told at an unconscious level in the adult characters' lives. The last scene, because it is unexpected, lifts the energy curve at the end of the play, without using a conventional happy ending.

I thought of the women as four musical instruments. If one scene is a duet, the next will be for three voices. It is easy to write a string of two person scenes, but this makes a dull rhythm, and the energy of the play drops.

Monologues

I use four monologues, or speeches, in *My Mother Said I Never Should*. In rhythm, each provides a resting place for the audience. In terms of storytelling, each monologue gives a character the chance to tell the audience a part of the story which the other characters do not know. This sharing of a secret brings us closer to that character. Rosie has the first monologue (p. 38–9) because she arrives in the adult scenes after the others, and this bonds her to the audience quickly.

In the première at Contact Theatre, Jackie did not have her long speech (pp. 83–4). Watching the performances, I realised there was a piece of the story missing because I had not given her a place in the structure to speak about the experiences she holds inside her for so long. And as this resting place was missing in Jackie's rhythm, she did not feel complete as a character. I added Jackie's monologue for the Royal Court production.

Emotional inheritance: a structure of advice

By emotional inheritance I mean the huge amount of information about our own past, and our family's past, which affects our energy and potential for change in each generation. This is *unconsciously* passed on in repeated behaviour, and *consciously* passed on in the form of advice. I use this handing down of advice to try and create a sense of generations of time and experience passing through the play. The impression of a sweep of time was one of the hardest things to create subtly and convincingly in the play.

Compressed into a single phrase of advice are huge clues about the attitudes of women, and of society towards women, in each generation. Doris takes Jackie outside to break two jam jars after she had broken a mug, because Doris has been taught:

> **Doris** Everything goes in threes. If you break one thing, more is sure to follow. (p. 14)

In the third child scene, when Rosie asks Jackie to look into the future for her, Jackie gives Rosie the advice she has picked up from Margaret:

Jackie It'll happen anyway. Mummy says don't cross bridges.
(p. 35)

At the end of the play, Jackie has changed this view, and discarded
her emotional inheritance:

Rosie Remember what Jackie said afterwards. We mustn't live in
the past. (p. 89)

Rosie is advising Doris on how to live after the death of her
daughter Margaret. In three generations we move from a
superstitious fear of the future, to a passive belief in fate, to a
rational view of life as one's own.

Emotional inheritance is mostly passed on unconsciously, and
this is expressed in the play by what I call the micro-structure.

The micro-structure

When I am writing a play it feels more like trying to construct a
globe, than making a flat script. In *My Mother Said I Never Should*
there are many cross-references joining scenes. The larger structure
of the play is concerned with contrast; whole scenes are juxtaposed
to show how different the women's lives are. The micro-structure
of the play is about connections, often ones the women are not
aware of. Internal desires join them across time.

The micro-structure may be in words which recur; in 1940 Doris
tells Margaret she is wrapping her up like a parcel (p. 12) when she
puts her to bed under the piano; Jackie says she wrapped up Rosie
in a shawl like a parcel when she brought her home from hospital
(p. 28). Ambitions connect; Margaret tells her mother Doris, on
the day she leaves home, that she will never have children (p. 30);
the same line is echoed by Rosie, two generations later, as she
leaves her mother Jackie (p. 84).

Micro-structure in performance and design

Most of the micro-structure is written into the play so that it will
appear in design and peformance, rather than in the spoken words.
The play is written for three dimensions.

Images recur; the moment of a daughter leaving her mother

forever happens three times in a garden – Margaret walking away from Doris (p. 33), Jackie walking away from Margaret (p. 20), and Rosie leaving Jackie (p. 84). In the child scenes, the emotional inheritance of women as a social group can be seen in the games the girls play. I write these images with lines of dialogue which tell an actor or designer what is happening in the space and action.

Gesture is a common and very theatrical way of showing how we repeat the habits of the previous generation – even when our words are rejecting their traditions. Act One, Scene Seven is a clear example of this; Margaret folds sheets with Doris in the manner women have done for centuries, while telling Doris how entirely different her life is going to be. I think about the gestures before I write the words which accompany, or contradict them. The actors can use these gestures in the play to indicate quickly the age or experience they have reached. Jackie and Margaret both set out as rebels when they leave home, but when we see them pick up a baby, or pack up crockery, we see how they have not shed their emotional inheritance.

Rosie's break with these traditions can be seen from the very first way she picks up the doll Suky. The behaviour towards Suky by three successive daughters demonstrates what each child has learned about the mother-daughter relationship. Compare nine-year-old Margaret with her doll in 1940 (pp. 9–13) with the way nine-year-old Jackie talks about the doll in 1961 (p. 23), and with eight-year-old Rosie's treatment of the doll (p. 38–9).

In this way objects dramatise the structure and themes of *My Mother Said I Never Should*. If the stage set is cluttered with many objects, the effect of the named objects will be drowned. Objects such as the transistor radio, the utility mug, the solitaire board, the piano stool, the cherry tree and Suky are used to enact the way past actions keep reappearing. The objects appear new in one scene, old and worn in another – the objects remind us that this is not a naturalistic play.

Certain costumes such as the ski-pants, the baby clothes and the engagement dress are written into the play's story. As these items reappear throughout the play they create a kind of theatrical magic, demonstrating visually how the past is continually alive, as when Doris's engagement dress appears as new at the end of the play.

The handing down of clothes from one generation to another is a particularly female ritual, and symbolises the process of emotional inheritance. Women's fashion works in cycles far more than men's fashion, so it is possible for the clothes to be rejected and then reclaimed, dramatising the women's attitude to their past.

Making patterns and repeating motifs is part of storytelling. One reason why I spent three years working over this play is that I was checking the cross-references whenever I moved a scene around, or even gave a character a new line of dialogue. Rewriting became like trying to rearrange the pieces of fruit in a trifle which has nearly set, without disturbing the whole.

Structure and plot

The landscape of this play is very ordinary in one sense, as I wanted it to be; lives we can all recognise, taking place in ordinary homes, around small incidents like lighting a birthday cake, folding washing or a child's painting. The structure makes these extraordinary, by using these incidents as the landmarks across an entire century. This is a big play, for mainstages. I wanted to dramatise how the decisions made by mothers have influenced each generation as much as wars or government policies.

Michael Attenborough, director of the Royal Court première :

> I think its greatest success (and one of the major reasons why I wanted to direct it) is that it is a political play with a small 'p'. It does not revolve around articulate, politically sophisticated, relatively liberated middle-class women; rather it focuses on perfectly ordinary people, facing common problems. The play packs a considerable punch, which springs from its ability to focus, economically and clearly, on the emotional highlights of women's lives, whatever their class and background.

A play has to make us want to know 'what happens next?' or we would all go home at the interval. Conventionally, playwrights have used a forward moving plot to keep our attention while they unfold themes and develop character. This has been the tradition from Greek drama, through Shakespeare, Restoration plays such as *The Country Wife*, and nineteenth-century plays by Shaw or Wilde.

Like many plays of the 1970s and 1980s this play explores how our lives don't run like plots, with neat beginnings and endings. This is a very twentieth-century attitude that started late in the nineteenth century with Ibsen and Chekhov.

In *My Mother Said I Never Should* structure replaces plot. It is not the story, but the order in which it is told, which creates dramatic energy and suspense. Through Act One, the audience witnesses all the family secrets of four generations, while the characters learn only a portion of these. The objects and confrontations of Act Two would not carry suspense and drama if we did not know the history attached to each one. So it is Act Three that tends to affect audiences most powerfully; not because the most dramatic incidents happen there, but because we know what is at stake behind every line, every decision.

The giving and withholding of information is a very different way of creating drama from the tradition of confrontation between characters, a climax, and a conclusion. In this play the audience is given secrets to hold, secrets which are needed to complete the meaning of subsequent scenes. The presence of the audience is needed to complete the story. I want to make plays which are not finished on the page, or in the rehearsal room, but only when the audience is present. At each performance, and in every person, the meaning is slightly different, and each one is valid. To me, this is what makes theatre 'live', unlike a novel, film or television play.

Some of the meaning of scenes comes retrospectively. Because of the structure, we have one set of responses as we watch a scene, and another response later, when a new scene tells us more about what was happening to the people in that earlier scene. Rather than showing cause then effect, as in a play like *Macbeth*, the structure of *My Mother Said I Never Should* shows effect before cause. Three consecutive scenes in Act One demonstrate this process.

In Act One, Scene Five, Margaret suffers a miscarriage:

Doris If you hadn't been so hasty to get that temping job, you would never have lost the baby. (p. 23)

Immediately following, in Scene Six, but ten years later in time, Margaret addresses her own daughter Jackie who is also caught in the dilemma between having a baby and having a career:

Margaret Why did you have to try! . . . A year ago you had everything, you were so excited about the art school, new friends, doing so well. (p. 26–7)

Both mothers believe their daughter is ruining her chances as a woman. But there has been a change in the definition of a successful woman; Doris believes dedication to a baby comes before any work outside the home; Margaret believes Jackie should not keep her baby when she could make a career. However, these present time opinions are the result of their own histories, which we only learn in Scene Seven. Margaret is about to leave home, twenty years earlier:

Margaret I'm not going to have a family, babies and all that. Ken and I have decided. (p. 30)

We also learn about the beginning of this saga:

Doris What makes you think I wanted children?

Margaret Mother!

Doris I had a job too. I know it was only teaching, but . . . There wasn't any choice, then. p. 31)

So the structure shows us how Jackie is persuaded by Margaret to give up her baby for her career (Act One, Scene Six), before we learn the cause; that both Margaret (Scene Five), and even Doris (Scene Seven), lost this opportunity for themselves when the moment of choice arrived. The structure is political, in the sense that it shows how we limit ourselves by repeating a negative attitude to change. Both Doris and Margaret scold their daughters at the exact moment the daughter needs support. I write for emotional as much as political effect, and it made me cry to write these scenes where the inability to give love prevents the behaviour of a family or society from changing. I want a scene to affect me this powerfully when I write it, because then I feel it will affect the audience as powerfully when it is recreated by the actors in performance.

In Scenes Five and Six we see three generations; the mother and daughter react consciously to each other while the granddaughter is affected unconsciously. Rosie may not consciously remember being given away in Scene Six, but when she discovers it as an adult she realises she always knew. As she says to Jackie:

Rosie (*pause*) I used to hate you, only I never knew why. (p. 84)

Similarly in Scene Five, Jackie as a child witnesses the central conflict in a woman's life – baby or career. Jackie absorbs the fact that her own mother's choice may have lost Margaret her baby. By placing this directly before the scene in which she hands her own baby to Margaret, the structure reflects the major theme of the play; how our unconscious memory is at work in our present day decisions – how a woman is the product of her mother, and *her* mother before her. So in Scene Six, as we watch Jackie give Margaret her baby, we are aware that she may be unconsciously replacing the lost baby of Scene Five.

There is a question carried by the structure as to how much every woman, in every scene, is trying to get her mother to listen to her and love her. Ironically it is Rosie who, cut off from this relationship at birth, is given the love of three 'mothers', and feels free to make her own way. This breaks a chain going back to Doris's mother, who is the person being addressed at the very end of the play.

Doris's last speech

This last speech is not placed at the end for nostalgia, but for irony. The irony comes from the placing of the speech in the structure, not from the words of the speech. It needs to be performed innocently to heighten the irony; and joyously to bring up the energy at the end of the play.

The form of the speech is the archetype of a daughter asking to be loved and her mother being unable to love her, and in this way it sums up the dynamic of the play.

The content completes the story of Doris's life and reveals how she and Jack loved each other when they met. The structure of the play has already shown us how they all but allowed society's definitions of work and family to crush their spontaneity, in trying to conform to their generation's idea of a good woman and man.

The rhythm of the speech begins in a rush of excitement. But Doris falters, increasingly nervous as her mother refuses to answer.

Doris hesitates over the word 'love' and cannot say the word 'marriage' because she suddenly realises that her mother did not have the choice of marrying or giving up work, but raised her daughter alone. Doris realises at this happiest moment in her life, the full extent of her mother's unhappiness. Her mother's silence conveys the envy passed on from mother to daughter. Doris stumbles on this at a moment when she cannot confront it, because she is vulnerable – she wants her mother's blessing. Like Margaret and Jackie, at the moment when the daughter seeks her mother's approval to be different, she realises there is jealousy where there could be love.

I wrote the last speech very early on in the first draft, knowing that this would be the ending of the play.

Structure and expectations: Giving away the baby

There is a pattern of expectations set up through the play, the expectations are broken, and then set up again, until each mother learns to let her daughter go. The expectations may be as small as Doris wanting Margaret to have clean hands and a tidy dress to play the piano but they web the play. When Margaret comes to tell her widowed mother that her marriage is breaking up, Doris advises:

> **Doris** You expected too much. So did I. And Jackie expects even more. (p. 70)

What they expected, was the traditional goal: happiness through marriage and motherhood. When each woman is disappointed, she carries the expectation over to her daughter, and tries to get her daughter to fulfill the happiness she seeks. So it is in Act One, Scene Six, that Margaret tries to persuade Jackie to look for happiness in a career; the option that Margaret lost:

> **Margaret** (*gently*) You've got such opportunities.
>
> **Jackie** Expectations.
>
> **Margaret** Yes!
>
> **Jackie** Yours. (p. 27)

In this crucial scene of the play, Jackie is persuaded by Margaret to give up Rosie – actually not so much for Jackie's sake but for Margaret's and for generations of women.

> **Margaret** You've got to go further than me – and Rosie too. (*Quietly.*) Otherwise . . . what's it been worth? (p. 28)

The enormous sacrifice of Jackie's generation is to relinquish motherhood for the career world. Denied motherhood, she is, strangely, the only mother who gives her daughter love without jealousy. Is it because Jackie's identity is not defined by her success as a mother, or wife? Or is it because she does not expect her daughter to love her? Doris is wrong; Jackie does not expect more, it is the other women who expect more of Jackie. Jackie herself does not expect to be happy. She expects to work.

The chain is broken through the character of Jackie. It is easy to see this character as selfish or unfeeling – as women of the seventies and eighties have been dubbed. I wanted to write about such a woman, slightly older than me, so as to understand what she carries inside her.

Rosie is a few years younger than me. She is born at the end of the century, a time when most of the expectations for women have been challenged. It is easier for Rosie to reject the emotional inheritance which constrains women – in the same way that she leaves the packing up of the room in Act Two to Margaret and Jackie. The older women are seen doing the hard work to free the woman of today. Rosie mistakenly concludes:

> **Rosie** . . . I've discovered the secret, all by myself! (p. 91)

As Rosie speaks, sitting at the solitaire board, the structure delivers us the whole picture. Four present tenses become visible at once; Jackie and Margaret appear upstage, looking as they did in the scenes where each lost Rosie. Rosie is still onstage. Doris runs on, not much older than Rosie:

> **Doris** . . . I'm so happy, SO HAPPY! I suppose, really and truly, this is the beginning of my life! (p. 92)

As Doris speaks of her expectations for the future, the structure offers a last question. Here are two young women, sixty years apart, standing in almost the same backyard in Oldham. Doris appears very happy, talking of her husband to be; Rosie looks 'like a victim' (p. 90) in her messy clothes, and knows she is alone – she is setting the marbles on the solitaire board for a new game. Rosie has no inherited expectations, Doris had traditional ones. Why don't we create the lives we set out to find? And is it possible that daughters have to release mothers from the need for their approval, as much as the other way round?

John Peter, reviewing the 1987 première in the *Sunday Times*, concluded that the play is about 'how it takes generations to learn about the value of real feeling'.

The Child Scenes

In the *Independent* in 1989 Paul Taylor described the child scenes as 'dream-like interludes . . . gimmicky and melodramatic by comparison with the solid authenticity of the rest'.

The child scenes explore sex, death, gender, courtship, destiny and loneliness.

The language and body language of children is more dramatic than that of adults; and more entertaining (see Appendix: Exercise 1). This does not mean the scenes should be performed as child*ish*. I wanted to show how, inside the adult, the child is shouting what the adult may refuse to hear (see Appendix: Exercise 2).

In my mind's eye, when I was writing the play, the child characters were huge. This happens in performance, because the children are not played by child actors, but by adults. I wanted to show older faces and bodies becoming children again to dramatise how the child is still alive inside the mother, or grandmother (see Appendix: Exercise 3). As played by adults, the child scenes are part of the way I am trying to challenge our preconceptions about people. If children played the child scenes, the irony would be lost. The child scenes establish that the play is not entirely naturalistic.

Children ask questions which adults have been trained not to:

Margaret . . . What happens when you die?

Doris (*long pause*) I'll bring you some cocoa presently. (p. 12)

Margaret is still asking this question as an adult, in her dying scene where she wanders through her unconscious, and back into her child self (p. 81). Children ask the unanswerable questions.

The Wasteground: a magic place

I decided at the very beginning of writing *My Mother Said I Never Should* to use child scenes to expose the unconscious of the play. And so all other scenes take place on the wasteground space. I don't ask for a set for the adult scenes, but for certain props to be laid on the ground, just as the children lay out the sticks and sweet papers in the first scene 'To call up . . . spirits from beyond the grave' (p. 7). Theatrically, this makes a visual statement about the root of all the adult behaviour. To say that some scenes are fantasy and others authentic, seems odd to me, as all the scenes in the play are fantasy.

The child scenes introduce magic. The children repeat words, searching for the secrets of adulthood in the most ordinary phrases, like 'Don't cross bridges' (p. 35) I am interested in female magic, the witch in women, that has been condemned for centuries:

Jackie See? Proves it. Our powers.

Doris What powers?

Jackie In the earth.

Rosie What happens to people when they die then?

Jackie They rot. Worms go in their nose and out their eyeballs.

Doris No! (*Starts to cry.*) Don't want to do that – (p. 80)

This female magic is not childish, it is about huge and sometimes harsh realities. Everything comes from the earth of the wasteground in *My Mother Said I Never Should*, and returns to it. The wasteground is an uncompromisingly real place, and a magic place where things can happen. The children have this ability to deal with the real and unreal together because they are not self-conscious. I set the wasteground well away from the adult world, and from boys, to show that girls are not born good.

Sometimes people tell me that Jackie's line 'Let's kill our Mummy' (p. 5) proves that Jackie 'kills' Margaret in the course of the play. To me this indicates we are all more interested in magic than we confess; people are suggesting that a wish spoken by a child makes someone die, years later.

The child in the adult

The idea of examining the behaviour of the child to understand the adult runs through much twentieth-century psychology, and even appears in the Bible. I was not aware of this when I wrote the play. The child scenes seemed to me the most theatrical and direct way of revealing complex ideas. Other women playwrights such as Sarah Daniels, Caryl Churchill, and Sharman MacDonald use child characters in adult plays – more than our male colleagues seem to do. Perhaps, as women, we are not so pressurised into obliterating the child in ourselves, so we tend to use it more as a reference point.

Jenny Howe, who played Margaret in the 1987 world première at Contact Theatre, Manchester:

> The driving force of the play is the children. The child scenes *energise the play*. And you think, what would other plays be like, if you saw Hamlet with his Lego, or Medea with her dolls. It's true, we do still have the child in us though we may deny it, and the child tells us so much about the adult.

Themes in the child scenes

Each child scene sets up a major theme of the play. The only chronological storytelling runs through the five child scenes. A thematic cycle is set in motion in this way by each child scene; as it is completed, the next taboo is raised.

The emotional inheritance of women is introduced in the first child scene in two opening rhymes, and the desire to change this follows with the line 'Let's kill our Mummy' (p. 5)

The question of how to be a woman is a continuous thread through all the scenes, changing colour between child and adult scenes, but passing unbroken from one character to another. Every scene in the play begins and ends with a line which bounces off the one before, and the child scenes are part of this ironic structure. For example in the second scene when Doris wants to play at babies, Rosie warns:

> **Rosie** You have to get married first. (p. 18)

The scene changes and we see Margaret as a flustered mother, embarrassed and horrified by her teenage daughter's sexual adventures:

> **Margaret** (*switches off the transistor*) I should never have let you go to that party in Hammersmith! (p. 19)

Jackie sprawls on the grass, a flagrant rebel. The taboos and fears about becoming a mother, let loose by Doris and Rosie in Scene Three, run through the next four adult scenes. The warning of Rosie's line 'You have to get married first', comes home to roost in Scene Six, where we see Jackie struggling as a single mother, and Margaret unable to accept the situation.

The third child scene plays with betrayal in relationships. Jackie and Rosie play games about secrets, lies and the promises made – and broken – by girls and boys. Scene Nine follows with how the adults deal with this; the arrival of baby Rosie is masked by a telephone call conducted in the adult language of fibs and banalities. The secret festers through Act Two and into Act Three, until the outburst between Jackie and Margaret in the office, over who Rosie belongs to.

The fourth child scene, Act Three, Scene Three, stares into the cauldron of mortality:

> **Jackie** You can't make someone's life go backwards. (p. 80)

Adult Jackie still hasn't learned, or will not hear, what child Jackie knows. The juxtaposition of the child with the adult heightens the tragedy of lost relationships, lost communication.

The fifth child scene looks over the edge of death. The voice of the child goes on asking questions, inside the head of her daughter.

Catharsis in the child scenes

In structural terms the child scenes are built into the play at five points when a change of energy and pace are needed. They provide a bolder level of humour and horror, which releases the emotional tension of the adult scenes – both for the actors and for the audience. We can react more freely to the child scenes, just as the characters react more freely to events.

For example, in Act One, Scene Two we see a mother and daughter in the dark of an air raid, too fearful and tense to know how to express their sexual anxieties or emotional needs. Scene Three is a rude and boisterous exploration of these sexual taboos – done in such a way that the audience can laugh, even though the images the children produce are quite disturbing (see Appendix: Exercise 4).

However, it is very important that the child scenes are never performed for laughs. These children have run away to a dark patch of land beyond the sight and rules of adults, to touch what girls are not supposed to even know about.

Taboos

Jackie (*can't bear it any longer*) Let's kill our Mummy. (p. 5)

I have been told that this idea is unnatural, or that Jackie must be disturbed. Personally, I think almost everybody has played childhood games which begin something like: 'Let's pretend our parents are dead and we're orphans.' Then the business of exploring the universe can really begin. This is how the child scenes are introduced – in fact, how the play is introduced. The children are prepared to set off on the most frightening journey there is – into all the taboos, alone. They take us with them. It seems to me that it is only when we stand alone that we discover how to live, and love; as adult Rosie discovers at the very end of the play.

Jackie speaks the line because my intention was to show she is the bravest, in that she voices what the others want. We have to look at the context of any line in a play to see what it responds to. After singing 'My Mother Said I Never Should', none of the children wants to conform to the definition of girls as 'Sugar and spice and all things nice'. They want to kill their ancestors, the Mummies who have bequeathed them this emotional inheritance.

Jackie is brave enough to speak the line, but you cannot be brave unless you are also afraid. Courage in girls is often read as unnatural or unfeeling, where it would be admired in a boy. It is easy for audiences to disapprove of her as we often criticise women who are not self-sacrificing. The mechanism of this in the play is that the other characters gradually disown Jackie, after daring her to do for all of them what none would dare to do themselves – in both the adult and the child scenes:

Doris Stop it!

Rosie Stop the spell.

Doris Make it go backwards.

Jackie You can't make someone's life go backwards.

And as the others run off, leaving her in the dark, Jackie cries:

Jackie I didn't mean to do it! Don't leave me all alone! (p. 80)

If we blame Jackie, we use her as the others do; to carry the conflicting feelings we would rather not own.

The child characters

While the child scenes operate as the unconscious of the play, the child characters are the core material of the adults. Their ages correspond to the amount of obligation they carry; Doris is the baby, Margaret and Jackie both nine, Rosie eight.

Doris is never quite sure what is happening, and goes along with the others' decisions. Likewise, as an adult of that generation, she is the most naïve in the play. Her life choices were limited in comparison to those of Margaret and Jackie, so she never understands some of the pressures they experience. The very old and very young are often excused of responsibility in the same way. In the child scenes Doris is shooed away as a nuisance, which is what I imagine Jackie and Margaret would like to do to Doris at the beginning of Act Two. In this way the child scenes act out the subtextual desires of the play.

I also made Doris the baby to give the actress who plays Doris some scenes where she is liberated from being the oldest in the play. When I am writing I try to think about what is interesting for the actor, as well as for the play. Joan Campion, who played Doris in the world première at Contact Theatre, Manchester:

I was already well into middle age when I played Doris but I really felt so at home being a child again. I wanted to *play* as a little girl – I don't think I had had my fill of it. The war and the sense of doing the right and sensible thing shortened the childhood of Margaret's generation and mine.

Rosie wants to experiment; with sex, death and birth. She is interested in touching blood, bodies, the voodoo sticks and sweet papers. She plunges into the sensory experience, where Jackie is aware of the spiritual force. As adults we see how Rosie is not afraid of expressing her feelings, while Jackie is anxious about what people will think of her. Rosie's uninhibited reactions are partly what helps her survive the great shocks she has as a teenager. Jackie's child carries responsibility for the others and for decisions, much as she does later for the family in the adult scenes. She doesn't express fear until left alone.

Margaret's child is anxious, hovering around the voodoo, interested, but afraid to try things. Margaret and Jackie are both the same age as children; the oldest and most serious. Margaret needs Jackie, from the first scene of the play, when they discuss killing Mummy:

Margaret (*to* **Jackie**) Dare you!
. . . Do mine! – I don't like blood . . . (p. 6)

It is this same voice in adult Margaret which persuades Jackie to act out her own desires:

Margaret You've got to go further than me . . . (p. 28)

Ultimately, child Margaret recognises this and acknowledges child Jackie for her courage in a way which does not happen in the adult scenes. In the last child scene, after adult Margaret has died, Jackie thinks she has lost everyone:

Jackie They wanted me to kill you.

Margaret It didn't work.

Jackie Sure?

Margaret Yes.

Slight pause.

Jackie The others won't play with me any more. (p. 85)

Margaret has crossed the golden river – the line of death, among other things. She invites Jackie to her secret hide. But Jackie chooses to go back – an act of separation from her mother's wishes which she has so far never achieved in the play:

Jackie No. I have to go back. – Do you mind?

Margaret *shakes her head.* **Jackie** *lets go of her hand and walks away. The lights start to fade on* **Margaret,** *who stands watching until* **Jackie** *is out of sight.* **Margaret** *resumes balancing along the cracks in the paving.*

Margaret King of the Golden River . . . I'm the King. (p. 85)

Margaret's death has released Jackie, but Margaret has not abandoned her. If I wrote the scene between their adult selves, it would have to be naturalistic; I could not show people who are both dead and alive. The scene would have to be either a farewell or a reconciliation, it couldn't be both. I felt this would be sentimental or contrived. Children use language full of symbols and poetry with a lightness that we hardly ever regain; it is not self-conscious.

The child scenes form a landscape in which the women exist outside of all other times in the play.

Language

Words in *My Mother Said I Never Should* are for lies, secrets, spells, and for not saying what one means. Words are used to express the invisible; either information about the past or future, which cannot be shown; or psychological information, which usually contradicts what a character is telling us through her face and body. I wanted to use a triangle of contrast between what is seen, what is spoken, and what is meant (the subtext). This sets up a continuous circuit of suspense.

Although the language is very ordinary, in the sense that it is everyday vocabulary, it not naturalistic. Clichés and everyday conversation are compressed and heightened. Several power exchanges are happening under every line:

Margaret It's funny, Mother, Jackie and Rosie don't even like cocoa.

Doris You only want what you're denied. (p. 48)

On one level this is a banal exchange between two of the four
women packing china. However, Margaret's line about her
mothering of Rosie and Jackie makes a reference to a past time
when she was neglected by Doris. Although the pain of this past
moment is not apparent, the audience have witnessed this moment
(Act One, Scene Two) so they understand this subtext, and can
also observe that Jackie and Rosie do not. In this way subtext in
the play often enables two characters to talk secretly in front of a
third party. Margaret is also asserting that she is the mother of
both Jackie and Rosie, in the way she refers to them in one breath;
subconsciously Margaret is always trying to convince herself, and
the others, that she is the mother of Rosie. Words are spells,
repeated they have an effect. If Margaret paused before 'Rosie' or
there was a dash to indicate an afterthought, Rosie would pick this
up as meaning uncertainty, and probably question it. The line is
also a statement of fact about the different generations and their
tastes.

Doris's reply could be delivered simply as the advice of an old
woman. However, it is a bleak reply to a line which seemed quite
mild, suggesting that Doris has picked up the sting in Margaret's
observation, and is defending herself. Because the phrase is
generalised, Doris may be referring to her own memories of being
neglected by Jack, as much as to Margaret's memory of being
neglected by Doris.

Words and characterisation

The choice of words tell us the age, status, upbringing, politics and
sense of humour of the speaker. I did not realise the degree to
which the words in the play are used as codes, until it came to be
translated into other languages. The Swedish translator telephoned
me with problems translating the line:

> **Doris** . . . I may be as old as the Queen Mother, but *I* buy all my
> smalls in Top Shop. (p. 88)

'I may be' is half question, half statement. This phrase colours the
rest of the line; different performances can make Doris appear
ironic, teasing, prim or serious, depending on the delivery of three
words. 'As old as the Queen Mother', tells us Doris's age. It also

conveys her politics; she has given herself status over younger generations by aligning herself with the oldest member of an ancient English institution. However, with the line 'But *I* buy all my smalls in Top Shop', Doris implies that she is more self-reliant and up to date than the Royal Family. The stress on '*I*' defines her sense of superiority, so the stress is marked. The stress on one word can give the actor the clue to a whole character.

'Smalls' is the idiom of an older woman, probably from the North of England. An audience could guess that it means underwear because it is visually descriptive. Dialect words are often naturally poetic in this way, and I like using them. The echo with 'small' also suggests modesty; while the sound of 'Top Shop' suggests brash 1980s high street fashion. The actor can use the snappy 'p' sounds to heighten the comic contrast. Thus Doris switches from being a demure woman to a teenager in one line. The actor will know this is intentional, not a mistake on Doris's part, because of the parallel action; Doris unpeels her stockings, and puts on mirror sunglasses. She intends to amuse us. She is playing with preconceptions about old and young women, and she does it through words. Languages labels us, and if we change a word, we can change who we are.

For British audiences, 'Top Shop' sets the scene in the mid-eighties. In a play which jumps time and place, a single word or brand name can announce the period of a scene, such as the use of 'Austin Healey' (p. 31) instead of simply saying car.

Four languages

Each woman speaks in a different vocabulary and speech rhythm, according to her generation and place of upbringing.

The four vocabularies are clearly established in the opening scenes where each child speaks of her Mam, Mother, Mummy or Mum. This instantly establishes the conflicts of age, class and status which run through the play.

Jackie She's my Mummy.

Doris I'm her Mummy.

Jackie Yes but she calls you 'Mother'. That's different.

Doris How?

Jackie Just is. (*Pause.*) (p. 13)

The different vocabularies also inject energy and humour into the lines. I wanted the dialogue to be as musical and acute as poetry. So I chose words for their performance quality as well as their meaning. Words such as wally, scrimping, choc-a-block, piggy, housewifery, kazooming, actually, umbrage, dazzling, hasty and yucky, give the actors as much scope for characterisation as whole speeches. (See Glossary for meanings.)

The *rhythm* in a line of speech indicates a character's intentions and aspirations. This is one reason why the meaning of a line of dialogue cannot be fully understood until it is spoken aloud. For example, all the children, and Rosie, use short sentences which express directness of feeling. The other women rarely use these, except when upset or angry. However, when Rosie returns from her holiday with Jackie, and wants to sound more adult and sophisticated to Margaret, she uses longer and more complex sentences (pp. 71–3). When I was writing the play I tried the lines aloud to myself all the time.

Each character's vocabulary and rhythm changes as the character grows older. This is one way a scene is located in time; it also gives the actor the means to pace her performance. Like a singer, the actor does not want to reach the high notes too soon.

Maintaining the four languages authentically and weaving them into one dialogue was one of the hardest aspects of writing *My Mother Said I Never Should*. I didn't use books to research vocabulary or dialect because I thought this would sound wooden when spoken. For years I had lived in Manchester and Leeds listening to women of all ages and experiences talking. I wrote the play by drawing on an unconscious pool of memories. This doesn't mean that the lines in *My Mother Said I Never Should* are taken directly from life. What I absorbed over the years was how it feels to *be* other kinds of women, rather than how to copy them. I find playwriting close to acting, because I have to get inside the character I am writing, then the words will come out convincingly (see Appendix: Exercise 12).

Myth not documentary

The dialogue of the play is not documentary or naturalistic. I felt that much of the writing in the first wave of plays by women, written between the 1960s and early 1980s, had a documentary quality. By contrast, I wanted to use language to reveal the imagination of women. Some of the lines which sound like old sayings are entirely made up:

> **Doris** Work hard and you will rise like bread, my mother said. (p. 59)

Each woman uses language to weave a myth about her life and identity. Doris, being the oldest, shows most clearly how the telling of one's life story is embellished and exaggerated with time. The passage in Act Two where Rosie and Doris polish the piano together exposes this process, because Rosie challenges the 'myths' Doris tells, and Doris herself reveals the way we mythologise the past:

> **Doris** . . . the girl next door was illegitimate too, it was more common than they put on those documentaries. (p. 59)

It is important that the actors do not deliver the dialogue of the play as pure reminiscence. There is always a game being played by at least one woman onstage; language is her costume.

Clichés and avoidance

One kind of mask in language is the use of cliché. Margaret and Jackie speak in clichés when they discuss sex (pp. 19–20) as do Doris and Margaret in 1951:

> **Doris** Mother Nature is very hard to fight. It's not just a question of rubber things, or what have you. (p. 31)

I like using clichés because they are a costume language we all recognise and use when a subject or situation is too difficult to find a language for. They are dramatic because they expose the gap between what is spoken and what is meant. The plays of Willy Russell use this device, most notably in *Shirley Valentine* where cliché is used to show an 'ordinary' woman struggling to express questions of love, death and destiny.

Clichés are hard to argue with; they are familiar and so sound like truths. Thirty-six years after the above scene, Doris and Margaret meet when both their marriages have finished. Neither of them can play the role of good wife or good mother any more, so they are finally able to talk about sex in their own, personal language:

> **Doris** Your Father . . . stopped 'wanting' me, many years ago. One didn't divorce, then. I thought if I persisted in loving him . . . I wanted to – to be desired. (*Pause.*) (p. 70)

The language is clumsier, the sentences are broken and hesitant; they indicate how Doris is searching for meaning, and how she speaks from emotion. In fact, in the same scene, Doris makes mockery of the polite, restrained language with which women are supposed to express themselves:

> **Doris** I ate my shoe this afternoon.
>
> **Margaret** Yes.
>
> **Doris** Margaret, you're not listening to a word I'm saying. (p. 69)

Compare this painfully truthful scene with the language Margaret and Doris use in Act One, Scene Nine; a telephone conversation where both women speak in clichés and keep to a pattern of questions and answers they obviously use every week. Both give short answers, and speak tangentially any time the conversation appears to be becoming emotional. Yet they understand from each other that Jack is dying, that something has happened to Jackie, and that something has changed in Margaret's life. They simply don't have the language to talk about it.

Humour in language

Words create humour from the image they suggest, such as Doris describing Jack as 'creeping' (p. 37), or simply from their sound, as in 'yucky anorak' (p. 55).

The child scenes should not be played for humour because this would upset the seriousness of their intentions. If we laugh it is because the children voice taboo subjects.

At moments when characters are trying to be very serious they use rather formal language. We laugh at the absurdity:

Margaret Mother can't possibly chew spare ribs. (p. 64)

Language such as this usually follows an intensely emotional crisis; here Rosie has discovered her baby clothes. If the audience laughs, this can be a way of acknowledging shock. In a play which shows some very traumatic moments, I wanted to use the opposite pole of humour as well. Sometimes humour heightens the tragedy. We often laugh at others' inability to communicate.

How actors discover the meaning of the dialogue

At school I was taught that proper use of grammar and dictionary definitions of words define their 'true' meaning. In spoken usage, it is the context of a word which defines its meaning. A word in *My Mother Said I Never Should* is given its meaning by the person who speaks it. The words 'thank you' are variously used as an insult, a reconciliation and a defence. The line

Jackie Whenever I can afford the fare to London (p. 28)

is used sincerely; in another scene it is used ironically:

Margaret Whenever you can afford the fare. (p. 73)

The word 'typing', as in Margaret's job, has a very different value when used by Margaret on p. 30 and by Rosie on p. 48. As a child, Jackie is aware of the dramatic conflict in words:

Jackie What's pampered?

Doris Nursed.

Pause. **Jackie** *looks at* **Margaret**. **Margaret** *looks at* **Doris**.

Margaret No, pampered is – being spoiled a bit – like you've been, here!

Doris Thank you, Margaret. (p. 22)

The meaning of words in the play is quite often different to their literal meaning. An example is when Rosie asks Doris for her opinion about a painting by Jackie:

Doris (*pause*) I like the gold frame. Looks expensive. (p. 87)

I wanted to use a theatrical language which illustrated how often women seem to deny what they are feeling. Michael Billington summed this up in his *Guardian* review of the Royal Court production in 1989:

> Ms Keatley has realised that the characteristic sound of English family life is of people telling each other evasive untruths.

Fibs are also more fun for the actor and audience than the one-dimensional truth.

Acting the pause

The pauses in the text of the play are always as important as the words themselves to indicate meaning to an actor. There are slight pauses, pauses and long pauses marked in the text. Sometimes these begin a line, sometimes they break a line. I try and use pauses instead of stage directions. A pause indicates that a line is not to be delivered straight, but does not tell the actor how to deliver it. A pause gives the actor a space in which to enact the character's intention in whatever way she decides to interpret it. There is also a silence marked after Rosie shows Jackie she has discovered her birth certificate (p. 83).

Stage directions

If it is essential to the meaning of a scene that a line is delivered in a particular way, the stage direction will specify that information. There is a balance in scenes between lines which are statements of emotion or fact, and ambiguous lines which can be played against the facts.

Because *My Mother Said I Never Should* does not use scenery to show time and place the first lines of every scene function like verbal stage directions to the audience. However, these lines are not simply factual but indicate the status and emotional issue of the scene:

Rosie Morning post, Mrs Metcalfe. (p. 71)

I tried to make these opening lines humorous to give the actor something more than a lump of information to play with:

Margaret I should never have let you go to that party in Hammersmith! (p. 19)

Playing with punctuation and grammar

In rehearsals for the Contact Theatre première, Brigid Larmour and I debated the commas, semi-colons, full-stops, dashes and dots wherever I had used them. These are a writer's tools for signalling the timing of lines.

I don't understand theories of grammar, but we all use them in practice. Language in plays is most revealing when it breaks all the rules of grammar, like the dialogue in Beckett's or Pinter's plays.

When Margaret arrives to take baby Rosie from Jackie, the grammar and punctuation guide the actors into playing the scene. The lack of nouns and pronouns, the dots and dashes (pp. 25–6), express the tension, awkwardness and uncertainty of the women. I was trying to write a scene which is almost unimaginable, and it took me nine drafts before I could invent the right language – which is a language of gaps and the unspoken, because there is no language for a mother giving away her child. There is no pattern of clichés that Margaret and Jackie can fall into, because they have gone over the edge of accepted female behaviour. When I felt I had the right draft, I knew from its shape on the page; a jagged poem with no rhythm or rhyme. In the second half of the scene, when the women talk about their own ambitions rather than about Rosie, the lines become longer and more articulate. The characters can fall into the language of mother and daughter again.

Female subtext: the violence of the play

I wanted *My Mother Said I Never Should* to show how violent women can be. But this is all expressed in subtext, because nice women aren't supposed to be angry. In their manipulation of words and subtext, I think women fight more cruelly than men – out of frustration at not being able to express their strength. Ken Olin, who directed the New York stage production in 1990, described the scenes as fencing matches where the women jab and parry with sharp lines, and these are punctuated by pauses where one is too wounded to continue for the moment. In America the tension and violence in the play has been more clearly perceived; perhaps women are more overt at expressing their anger in America.

To play the scenes, actors generally look for the conflicts underlying the words. The unspoken drama is what stops the apparently ordinary conversations being just that.

There are two vicious games in the play which recur through different generations. These are probably well known to psychologists. I didn't plan these, I was trying to write, dramatically, how I thought mothers and daughters often behave. I discovered the patterns of the play in rehearsal, as the actors do.

One game is a duel, where a daughter asks questions, and the mother refuses to answer. Act One, Scene Two is a clear example; Doris cannot and will not answer Margaret; although Doris as a grandmother will listen to, and answer, granddaughter Jackie. Charles Towers, director of the Boston première in America in 1993, pointed out to me how this dynamic continues right through the play to the very last speech, where Doris is asking her own mother questions, and is not answered. The mother feels the daughter is demanding and threatening, the daughter feels that she herself is not good enough.

Another game is challenges. One woman makes an emotional or factual statement as if drawing out her sword and holding it aloft. Another woman will strike at her statement. Another may come to her defence. Someone will raise another statement, and the round of battle finishes. Occasionally a truce is drawn. The women suppress huge battles under small fights, for example in Act Two, where Jackie tries to get Rosie back:

Margaret Everything in the binliner is for Oxfam.

Doris Nothing ventured, Jackie.

Jackie Mummy . . .

Margaret Jackie, if you're not doing anything, there's the spare room to sort out.

Jackie Yes, Mummy. (p. 56)

The fearlessness in Rosie's character is expressed in her language; she continues asking questions, past the point when the other women capitulate. Rosie is not intimidated if other women do not answer her.

Doris Well, Rosie will need bed linen.

Rosie What for?

Doris You never know.

Rosie I've got a duvet.

Margaret Rosie.

Rosie I have!

Jackie Rosie, why don't you and Granny go upstairs and sort out some sheets. (p. 49)

Rosie will not play the games. She uses reason where the others use subterfuge. It is amusing, and a relief, to have a character who breaks the game.

Female use of language

I kept the men offstage in order to show the way women use language, silence and subtext when alone together. The way men use language, silence and subtext has been well documented by centuries of plays where there are only men onstage. From Marlowe to Pinter there is a tradition of plays with no women characters, or where the women characters are written by men, for boy actors. Two contemporary plays which I think are brilliant depictions of male language and society are Trevor Griffiths' *Comedians* and David Mamet's *Glengarry Glen Ross*.

Although the language of *My Mother Said I Never Should* is clearly as recognisable to men as it is to women, I think that in this context the use of innuendo and subtext is profoundly female. I prefer this word to feminist; by female I mean an ancient and unconscious identity; 'Our powers in the earth' as Jackie calls them. The best way I can explain this is with the comments of a middle aged Manchester couple coming out of the Contact Theatre production. 'Oh I did enjoy that!' said the man. 'But you couldn't have enjoyed it as much as me,' replied the woman.

The language of children

> **Rosie** What happens to people when they die, then?
>
> **Jackie** They rot. Worms go in their nose and out their eyeballs.
>
> **Doris** No! (*Starts to cry.*) I don't want to do that – (p. 80)

The children use words to explore rather than avoid experiences. Odd then, that adults consider children's language to be fantasy. Perhaps when we laugh at children we are avoiding the questions they raise. Because their language is frank, it releases fears and emotions; in the child scene above, Doris expresses a fear she never voices as an adult, but which she passes on to her daughter:

> **Margaret** (*calls*) Mother – (*Pause.*) Mummy . . . (*Pause.*) What happens when you die?
>
> **Doris** (*long pause*) I'll bring you some cocoa presently. (*She goes.*) (p. 12)

By interspersing child with adult scenes, we see how the same person who can use direct language as a child, loses this articulacy on becoming an adult. Jackie is the most forthright speaker as a child, yet the most reticent about saying what she means, or asking for what she wants, as an adult.

The process of 'growing up' is supposed to make us more able to deal with the world, but as these women grow up, they adopt a language of avoidance and self-defence. *Fear* seems to be the key; suppressed fear makes the adult language false. Rosie maintains her self-expression. She is not brought up to be afraid of someone; it is the others who are afraid of her.

What I admire and wanted to use as a playwright is the poetic and imaginative use of words in children's speech. In the child scenes, the characters pick up sounds and play with them just as they play with sticks and games. 'Boiling oil', 'voodoo', 'séance', and 'Twickenham' are being used as much for their succulent sounds as literal meaning in Act One, Scene One.

However, the children have a strong sense of truth and fiction. When Rosie and Jackie make their vow of honesty (p. 34) the words are plain, and totally appropriate. When they weave a spell in a pretend cauldron (p. 79), Jackie is questioned by Rosie and Doris for using 'monkey's hat' and 'harelip', because the first is too unreal, the second too real. 'Poisoned dewdrop and tail of cat' are accepted. The children are never careless about words. Their games explore the power of words: 'I'm the King' (p. 85) announces Margaret; and if she says she is not dead, then she is not dead.

The children actually use logic and reason much more than the adults, and are frequently baffled by the way adults speak:

Jackie I think I'm in love.

Rosie How d'you know?

Jackie Because this boy made me cry. Daddy makes Mummy cry and she says it's because she loves him. (p. 34)

The children use language to pursue the truth. It is from adults that they learn to use language for subterfuge. As doctor and patient, Rosie and Doris adopt the coy tones and sexual innuendo of a woman and man:

Rosie I'll just have to feel it.

Doris (*jumps up*) Don't touch!

Rosie But you like it.

Doris I might catch a babby.

Rosie I think you've got one already.

Doris That's my husband's fault, you can't trust him.

Rosie How is your husband?

Doris Oh he's upped and gone.

Rosie Oh I am sorry.

Doris I'm not. You must drop by for a cuppa. That's enough now, your turn. (p. 17)

The punctuation indicates to the actors that Doris and Rosie do not fully understand *what* the lines mean, as they repeat parrot fashion. But they know *how* adults use language; for some kind of deceit. It is precisely when Rosie suggests Doris is pregnant without knowing about it that the language shifts from child frankness to adult slyness. They don't enjoy this, but feel obliged to learn how to do this. I set the child scenes well away from the adult world because I wanted to show that little girls are neither sweet nor manipulative until they are in the presence of adults who teach them to perform in certain ways.

Transformation through language

A family is like a small country, with its own language, rules and myths. Each member of the family in *My Mother Said I Never Should* is spoken to in a different way, which defines the role they have been allotted. To change their role, they have to change their language. Jackie expresses this as a teenager:

> **Jackie** If you want me to behave like an adult, then stop treating me like a child! (p. 19)

However, it is hard to break the language patterns we are taught. In Act Two, Jackie talks to Doris in the pacifying way that old people are often addressed:

> **Jackie** Sit down while the house warms up.
>
> **Doris** I don't want to be a nuisance to anyone. (p. 45)

Doris replies as an embittered old lady. Margaret speaks to Rosie in a similar language of directives which is used to control children; and she gets a childish response from Rosie:

> **Margaret** Rosie, bring that box over and start scrunching up newspaper for packing.
>
> **Rosie** (*kicking the box over to* **Margaret**) Do some chores instead. (p. 47)

Left alone together, Rosie and Doris talk to each other as equals, interested in listening to each other's opinions. Rosie immediately becomes more mature and Doris stops sounding senile – with neither losing the playfulness of the child inside.

> **Doris** They work too hard.
>
> **Rosie** You shouldn't wind them up.
>
> **Doris** You should be helping them.
>
> **Rosie** They'd only say I was more trouble.
>
> *They smile.*

Doris I'll show you something. (*Pulls the dustsheet off the piano from Act One.*)

Rosie (*pause*) It's the piano.

Doris Don't you like it?

Rosie We've got a synth at school.

Doris I had a friend called Cynth. (p. 57)

For me this is the pivot of the play; Rosie and Doris spot each other's games, and smile to acknowledge a truce. From these lines the actors playing Doris and Rosie can take their bearings on the rest of the scene, in fact the rest of the play.

Each character has a moment in the play where she speaks in language which is the same as her feelings, not a mask. This is a base point for the performer. It is Rosie who provokes the other women into saying what they feel:

Rosie My outside's the same as my inside. That's why when I talk Mum thinks I'm being rude. (p. 58)

This gift of Rosie's is simply the language of the child, which the others have lost – but can recover. Jackie is a very 'articulate' woman, but the hardest line for her to speak is:

Jackie (*hesitates*) I'm frightened. (p. 84)

Once a woman is using language true to her feelings, she is understood by others, even if her vocabulary and rhythms are entirely different. So it is that Rosie and Doris are not alienated by the different words 'synth' and 'Cynth' in Act Two as above. In the penultimate scene, Rosie and Doris swap advice on how to save money, dress, enjoy oneself or assess other people. Each woman speaks entirely in the language of her own generation. The delight is that they understand each other perfectly. They no longer speak and act as others want them to – the burden carried by Jackie and Margaret.

Language in families carries such strong preconceptions about people – who are discussed even before they are born – that it takes a great shock to break the patterns. Rosie is a catalyst who does not fit with any of the family roles and so opens the possibility for change. While everyone pretends that Rosie is

Margaret's daughter, the language the other women use towards Rosie reveals their uncertainty. They don't know what game to play with Rosie. Because Jackie can't exactly talk to Rosie as her daughter, nor as her sister, nor as a friend, Jackie listens to Rosie as a *person*, even when Rosie is only eight years old:

> Rosie . . . She always makes chocolate because she thinks I like it.
>
> Jackie Why don't you tell her you don't?
>
> Rosie Oh you know Mum. Never listens. I think she just likes making birthday cakes. Even Dad gets one!
>
> Jackie Let's light the candles.
>
> Rosie Shouldn't we wait for Mum?
>
> Jackie Oh, yes. (p. 39)

Jackie gives Rosie suggestions, not orders. She encourages Rosie to question Margaret about the cake, rather than succumb to a family ritual. Rosie feels equal enough to advise Jackie. In her language, Rosie mothers Jackie, who comes to Rosie for advice in Act Two, over the will, and in Act Three, when Margaret has died.

Spells

The language of the play has a magical quality; words, phrases, colours and images repeat. The language of the play is not naturalistic but a pool of incantations drawn on by different characters. Daughters vow never to have children, and grow up to hear their own daughters repeat the line. Sometimes a character is aware of invoking the words of another time and place, sometimes this happens unconsciously. The children in the adult scenes observe how there are actually more spells in the adult language than there are in the games of children:

> Doris Everything goes in threes. If you break one thing, more is sure to follow.
>
> Jackie Is that true?
>
> Doris So they say.
>
> Jackie Who's they? (p. 14)

The children explore their magic powers to create change. I think it is the adults' use of spells which is more frightening; the adults repeat spells to try and prevent change. Doris teaching Jackie to recite grace in French casts a spell over Margaret at tea. In Act Three when Jackie finally seems to be about to have Rosie back, Margaret summons the incantation of motherhood:

> **Margaret** Birthdays and first snowman and learning to ride a bicycle and new front teeth. You can't pull them back. (p. 77)

Talking with an Actor

Jenny Howe talks to Charlotte Keatley about her performance of Margaret in the first production of the play:

JH: My starting point for the character of Margaret was two scenes: Act One, Scene Two – Margaret's childhood in the war, with the cocoa, the piano playing, and the air-raid. We see her liveliness, her ability to be spontaneous and joyful, against her background; puritan. This is the start of her journey – and her inheritance.

The other marker scene for me was Act One, Scene Seven, where Margaret is folding the washing with Doris. Everything she talks about – going to London, typing, and not having babies – it's her fantasy of who she thinks she could be.

CK: Margaret has a lot of energy, and hope, in these scenes.

JH: Yet they show the battle; what Margaret dreams she could be, and what she is. She takes this battle through the play.

CK: I remember when Michael Attenborough was casting the Royal Court production, he said we mustn't cast someone who only shows the victim in the adult Margaret, but someone who shows us 'the woman wasted' – the joyful potential.

JH: That's why the child scenes are so important. I could bring out the playful Margaret that is locked away in the adult.

CK: As if she's taught that gaiety can't be part of real life.

JH: Or closeness. In the adult scenes the women are in constant battle – the child scenes bring them together, allow them to be close, and touch each other.

CK: How did you begin to play the child characters?

JH: Easy! Once you start to play games, you remember what it was like. Anyone doing this play should play children's games – skipping games, anything they can remember – play them around the text.

CK: I notice that in most productions, it's harder for the two younger actors to find the child.

JH: Yes, when we're younger, especially at teenage, we're still in a process of denial – 'I am not a child!' When you're a bit older you have nothing to lose and it's more fun and you're clearly an adult anyway.

CK: So you were playing the child scenes as funny scenes?

JH: No – the scenes are exploring childhood, not mimicking it. You have to remember from the *inside*, how serious things are when you're a child.

CK: Did you find it difficult saying lines like 'I'm never having any babies' when you know that Margaret does have children later on?

JH: It was important that we played the child scenes innocent of their characters in the rest of the play, and of what they would do as adults. Or you could spoil the magic.

CK: Did you find it hard to switch rapidly between child and adult characters, and adults of different ages?

JH: Each time I went onstage I would play each scene for all its worth and not think about how the play fits together. You can't play these scenes with irony – they would sound terribly symbolic, instead of being real people. You can feel the audience adding up the moments, it recognises what's going to happen next.

CK: How did you act the different ages?

JH: I found it essential to have fairly elaborate costume changes. It gives you the key physically, how to move.

CK: But you didn't change your make-up or hair, or use wigs.

JH: No. The adult scenes, like the child scenes, aren't about looking exactly like 1951. It's not a television play, it's a play about the essence of how we behave. You find yourself standing in the way your mother did when she was telling you off. The audience recognises that immediately, it's a quicker way of changing time period than elaborate sets or costume.

CK: What did you do about changing your voice between scenes?

JH: If you start by playing the action, the voice happens. Also if you start imposing on the voice, it doesn't work, it's a delicate thing. I think you could play Margaret with the same voice all through if the spirit was right.

CK: How did you find the spirit of the character?

JH: Joan Campion, who played Doris, and I, both felt we were playing our mothers! As an actress, this was an incredible way into the part. We were seeing events from the other side of the fence in a way we wouldn't in our own lives.

CK: Do you think Margaret takes baby Rosie from Jackie to try to resolve her own sense of loss? Or did you play Act One, Scene Six as if Jackie was giving her the baby?

JH: I think Margaret is still unresolved about taking Rosie, when Jackie phones her up. By the time she arrives at the flat she's drunk with the idea of taking the baby. It would be Margaret's second chance at motherhood.

CK: I visualised this scene like a see-saw.

JH: We played this scene on the edge, almost out of control.

CK: I wanted to show Jackie's exhaustion and loneliness and the reality of babies, rather than the symbolic or cute babies that tend to appear in plays – a woman holding a silent bundle.

JH: How to balance life between work and family – this still doesn't affect a man's life and career to the same degree. So babies don't come up in plays about men's ambitions. And I feel this hasn't been resolved or even helped by recent feminism. Men's lives haven't adjusted towards childcare, so how can women's.

CK: So is this a political play? Or a feminist one?

JH: It feels like Greek drama to act – Greek tragedy; people with their entrails being ripped out.

Feminist or Not?

It is mostly men who ask me whether this play is feminist or not. Scott McCormish who ran the pizza joint next to the theatre in Boston where the 1992 American première was launched, told me the audience reactions as they came in to eat every night:

> The women can't talk about the play enough, and the men who understand it love it, and the men who don't understand it are fearful of it.

When I wrote *My Mother Said I Never Should* I didn't think about whether it was feminist or not. I thought it was a play about life. Men have been visibly writing plays since Greek times, whilst plays by women have been extremely scarce. It is only since the 1960s that women have been visibly writing plays in substantial numbers. Some men confuse art and politics, and assume that all these plays by women must also be feminist. Charles Spencer, reviewing the 1987 Royal Court production in the *Telegraph*:

> For reasons that are no doubt impeccably feminist, Miss Keatley has banished all the male characters from her stage. Fathers and husbands are talked about but never seen, creating a curiously lopsided impression. It is as though she is favouring her audience with only one half of the story.

Surely such classics as Beckett's *Waiting for Godot*, Pinter's *No Man's Land*, Griffiths' *Comedians* and Mamet's *Glengarry Glen Ross* should also be labelled as 'lopsided impressions' of life, because only men appear in these plays?

I kept the men offstage in this play because I wanted female language and silence, humour, sexiness and violence, to walk onstage in a way which doesn't happen if men are present. Some men understand this perfectly. Alan Hulme, in his *Manchester Evening News* review of the 1987 première:

> Ms Keatley refuses to preach about a woman's nature and her place in the world, letting action and character speak for themselves . . . In this world men are banished off stage, out of sight, to cut the grass, but are rarely out of mind.

Women are used to seeing plays where men's lives are the metaphor for all people. Shakespeare wrote over thirty-five plays which, we are taught at school, cover all human experience. In fact, there is no Shakespeare play about a mother and daughter relationship, except *Romeo and Juliet*, but Juliet is brought up by her Nurse, and *A Winter's Tale*, where the mother is frozen during the twenty-five years of the play, so the King takes over. From reading classics, I understood that plays are metaphors; so I didn't write a play about four women to be read as for and about women. I saw the mother-daughter relationships as a *lens* through which to look at huge themes which concern all people. In his

Evening Standard review of the 1989 Royal Court production,
Milton Shulman decided otherwise:

> Ms Keatley manages to cram in a clutch of trendy and
> sentimental dilemmas that intrigue and bother the contemporary
> British female . . . the broken marriage, the generation gap, the
> single parent, the faithless husband, nursery games, family guilt,
> precocious intolerance and mother love.

Some men are so used to centuries of plays written by men, that
they seem unable to accept that women can write proper plays, or
plays about serious subjects which concern men too. I was told by
the literary director of the Royal Exchange Theatre and a BBC
producer in 1985, that my play was not a play, because of its
structure, and also that it wasn't about anything. Interestingly, no
female director or critic has dismissed the play on these grounds.
When the directors, actors, literary managers and critics of theatres
have been male, for centuries, some work by women may be so far
beyond the boundaries of their experience that they condemn the
experiment, before it is even staged. I think the label feminist may
be used for a play which breaks with tradition. That could even be
a play by a man.

This is why I didn't read Brecht or Stanislavski to help me write
My Mother Said I Never Should. I was trying to convert female
experience into theatre, so I had to invent my own conventions. It
is frustrating if this artistic innovation is confused with feminism. I
wish someone would write about the artistic movement of British
playwrights such as Caryl Churchill, Sarah Daniels, Anne Devlin,
Christina Reid, Sheila Yeger, Liz Lochead and many others who
are challenging and developing the art form of theatre, rather than
asking if we are feminist or not.

Why have there been so few women playwrights until now?
Partly it's due to their invisibility: if they're not published, it is very
difficult to rediscover them. But also, I think, it is because women
are educated not to raise their voice or opinions in public. Watch,
in a classroom, at a conference, in a television debate, or at a
family meal, whether it is the women or men who speak first, and
who tells the longest stories or jokes. Writing a play is daring to
provoke a public reaction. Since the 1960s, women have taken on
a public voice as journalists, politicians and playwrights.

Unfortunately the word feminist has been used to condemn such women as vindictive, humourless and bullying. I am proud to be called feminist if it means raising a voice that has not been heard, and therefore trying to redress a balance which has been a loss to men, as well as women.

After the 1992 American première in Boston, one man came up to me and gripped my hands:

> I'm seventy-four years old, I've learned more tonight than in my whole life so far, and my marriage matured tonight.

Another man was growling to his wife. He growled into my face:

> He should be locked up! The playwright, HE should be locked up!

I am a playwright because it is the best way I can respond to trying to live, now.

My Mother Said I Never Should

For

Hilda, Prudence, Susan, Victoria, Nicole
Joan, Jenny, Jane, Michele, Nettie
Judith, Shirley, Nancy, Linda
and especially
for Brigid, who made the play happen
and for Mum, who inspires me to communicate,
with love.

My Mother Said I Never Should was premièred at the Contact Theatre, Manchester on 25 February 1987. The cast was as follows:

Doris Partington   Joan Campion
  Born: Oldham, February, 1900. Engaged
  1923, married Jack Bradley in Oldham, 1924.
  (Age 5 in child scenes, as in 1905)
Margaret Bradley   .   Jenny Howe
  Born: Cheadle Hulme, April 1931. Married
  Ken Metcalfe in London, 1951. (Age 9 in
  child scenes, as in 1940)
Jackie Metcalfe   Jane Paton
  Born: London, July 1952. (Age 9 in child
  scenes, as in 1961)
Rosie Metcalfe   Michele Wade
  Born: Hulme, Manchester, September 1971.
  (Age 8 in child scenes, as in 1979)

Director and Dramaturg Brigid Larmour
Designer Nettie Edwards

A revised version of *My Mother Said I Never Should* had its première at the Royal Court Theatre, London on 23 February 1989, with the following cast:

Doris   Elizabeth Bradley
Margaret   Sheila Reid
Jackie   Jane Gurnett
Rosie   Shirley Henderson

Directed by   Michael Attenborough

The action takes place in Manchester, Oldham and London.

The setting should not be naturalistic. The design should incorporate certain objects which remain on stage throughout, such as the piano in Act One and Two, a tub of geraniums, a patch of wasteground. There are no sofas in this play. The setting should simply be a magic place where things can happen.

In the child scenes, each girl is dressed contemporary to her own generation, in the clothes each wears as a child in the 'real' time scenes, e.g. Margaret wears her Christmas frock, Jackie wears her 1961 summer dress.

There is an interval between Act Two and Act Three.

The solution to the Solitaire game is shown at the end of the play.

Act One

Scene One

The Wasteground, a place where girls come to play.

Enter four girls, each dressed contemporary to her own generation, singing:

My Mother said I never should,
Play with the gypsies in the wood,
If I did, she would say,
Naughty girl to disobey!

Rosie (*chanting*) What are little girls made of? (*Coaxing* **Doris** *to answer.*) Ssh . . .

Doris Sugar – and – (*Effort.*) – spice . . . ?

Margaret And . . .

Doris (*hesitantly*) And?

Margaret All Things Nice.

Doris *squirming, doesn't want to repeat it.*

Jackie (*can't bear it any longer*) Let's kill our Mummy.

Margaret Whose Mummy?

Doris Whose Mam? (*Copying.*)

Rosie Yes, whose Mum?

Jackie All our Mummies if you like?

Rosie Who's going to do it?

Margaret (*to* **Jackie**) Dare you!

Doris . . . Dare you . . .

Jackie We'll all do it.

Margaret It's my teatime . . .

Rosie How?

Jackie I dunno . . . Boiling oil.

Doris . . . Dare you . . . (*Repeating.*)

Margaret Shut up, baby.

Jackie Tell you what –

Rosie What –

Jackie I've got a penknife. I've been keeping it for something special.

Rosie You pinched it off Jimmy Tucker!

Jackie And we'll get some string, and take Mummy down by the railway line where there's a hole in the fence, and I think you have to put a stake through her heart.

Rosie We couldn't do them *all*. (*Pause.*) We haven't got enough string.

Jackie Just ours, then. (*Conspiratorial.*) They're not in our gang. Also they don't count because they're babies. They can do their own Mummys when they're old enough.

Margaret Do mine! – I don't like blood . . .

Jackie Lucy Parker cut her finger off at school.

Margaret I'll be sick.

Jackie Only the top bit. (*Pause.*) Like a flap.

Doris . . . Flip flap flop . . .

Rosie (*bends to* **Doris**) Do you want us to do your Mum?

Margaret She's too young to know.

Jackie She's got no Daddy: if we do her Mummy, she'll be an orphan and then we'll be responsible.

Margaret Her Mummy's all right – She gave us lemonade. (*Pause.*)

Rosie . . . She'll split on us though. Then we'll be outlaws.

Jackie Go away, baby.

Doris *cries.*

Jackie Go on. Go home. (*Pushes* **Doris** *away.*) Tea? Tea time.

All Tea time. Tea time.

Doris *goes.*

Jackie Piggy.

Margaret She'd only cry when she saw the blood. Me, I'm not having any babies.

Rosie How d'you know?

Margaret I'm not getting married.

Rosie (*pause. Thinks*). Well it still might grow.

Margaret What?

Rosie The seed. The baby seed, inside you.

Margaret It can't! Can it?

Jackie *has been arranging sweet wrappers.*

Rosie What are you doing?

Jackie Voodoo. We need bits of her fingernail and hair and stuff.

Rosie . . . She might haunt us . . .

Jackie You don't know *anything*, do you.

Rosie *is subdued.* **Margaret** *comes to look.*

Margaret What's that for?

Rosie Voodoo, you wally.

Jackie We're going to have a séance. To call up . . . spirits from beyond the grave.

Margaret We do that at school.

Jackie Do you?

Margaret On Fridays. Take buttercups apart, and count their . . . sta – stay – . . . bits.

Jackie Shh! Hold hands. (*They obey.*) You have to repeat after me.

Margaret
Rosie } After me.

Lights dim a bit.

Jackie (*deepens voice*) We call up the spirit of – Granny!

Rosie
Margaret } We call up the spirit of Granny!

Jackie Who died three years ago last Wednesday. And lived in Twickenham. Amen.

Margaret
Rosie } Amen.

Lights darken.

Margaret . . . It's getting dark . . .

Rosie . . . What happens now? . . .

Jackie (*deep voice*) YOU from beyond the grave! Tell us how to kill Mummy!

Lights almost blackout. Silence.

Jackie YOU from beyond the grave, tell us –

Margaret *and* **Rosie** *see something, scream and run off.*

Figure of **Doris** *now as Gran appears upstage, walking slowly towards them.*

Jackie Mummy! Mummy! (*Runs off after the others.*)

Doris *continues to walk forward, oblivious of above. She removes a dustsheet of World War Two blackout material from a large object which it has been completely covering. It is a baby grand piano.* **Margaret** *is crouching underneath it, hidden from* **Doris** *by a pile of bedding also under the piano.* **Doris** *begins to dust the piano as the lights rise for Scene Two and the wireless begins to play.*

Scene Two

Cheadle Hulme, Christmas 1940. **Doris** *is 40.* **Margaret** *is 9. The sense of a large front room, with austere decor. No Christmas* *decorations except for a vase of white, wax Christmas roses with a red bow, on the baby grand piano.*

Doris *dusts the piano lovingly. The wireless plays George Formby's 'Chinese Laundry Blues'. A pile of bedding is folded under the piano.*

Doris (*singing along*) 'Oh Mr Wu, he's got a naughty eye that flickers, you ought to see it wobble when he's ironing ladies' –

Margaret Knickers.

Doris Margaret? Margaret! Where – (*Goes to the wireless and switches it off.*) – Come out!

Margaret (*from the bedding under the piano, with a doll in her hands*) WHO was that?

Doris I have to listen to the wireless. In case Mr Churchill makes an announcement. It is my duty.

Margaret Knickers.

Doris Margaret. Come Out!

Margaret It was Suky.

Doris *walks around the piano.*

Margaret (*sings, at first softly*) Suky take it off again, off again, off again, SUKY TAKE IT OFF AGAIN –

Doris (*pulls her out from under piano by her arm*) Never, never!

Margaret Suky! (*Comforts the doll.*)

Doris I've told you before!

Margaret You've hurt Suky's arm! Torn her dress!

Doris (*shakes her*) Will you listen!

Margaret (*to the doll*) Suky don't cry. Mummy will cuddle you.

Doris I shall have to tell Father.

Margaret (*pause*) . . . Sorry.

Doris Pardon?

Margaret I'm very sorry Mummy.

Doris Mother.

Margaret (*pause*) Mother.

Doris And you've spoiled your frock. I'd just pressed that.

Margaret Haven't! . . . Yes I have.

Doris Have you done your practice?

Margaret (*trying a lie*) Yes. Bits of Chopin and Ten Very Easy Carols.

Doris *removes carol music from piano and replaces it with a piece of Beethoven music.*

Doris You ought to be on Beethoven now, not nursery rhymes. The amount we're paying for your tuition.

Margaret You're not throwing them away?!

Doris Of course not. They'll go to St. Mark's Jumble. Let me hear Beethoven's Minuet in G, Margaret. Have you washed your hands?

Margaret *holds out her hands, palms up and then palms down.*

Good girl.

Margaret *sits down at the piano and starts to play, very shakily, Beethoven's Minuet in G. She sways from side to side.*

Doris What on earth are you doing, Margaret?

Margaret I'm swaying with passion. Like the fat lady in the Hallé Orchestra.

Doris We'll have less passion and more perseverance, please.

Margaret *resumes playing. Sound of an air raid siren, distant. She plays on.* **Doris** *nods to emphasise the tempo.* **Margaret** *is still playing, but stumbling. Eventually:*

That will do nicely for this evening, Margaret. I think we shall get under the piano, now. Close the lid.

Margaret Next Door have got a proper Anderson shelter.

Doris (*miffed*) So shall we, presently. Father's been to the Depot but they've run out, had a pre-Christmas rush.

They arrange blankets, a quilt, a stone hot water bottle and a bolster. **Margaret** *hangs her Christmas stocking on the piano.*

Help Mother make the bed.

Margaret Watch out Suky, here comes a big fat bomb! Wheee! Eeee – oww –d–d–d–d–

Doris Margaret!

Margaret Well it looks like a bomb.

Doris It's a bolster.

Margaret I *know*, I – Suky thinks –

Distant rumble of aeroplanes which continues through the rest of the scene.

S . . . Suky wants a Christmas stocking too. She's not very . . . brave.

Doris Put your nightdress on.

Margaret Where's my gas mask?

Doris Here, see I'll put it by the bolster.

Margaret Where will you and Father sleep?

Doris In the hall.

Margaret Why?

Doris I think the ground floor is safest.

Margaret Why?

Doris (*pause*) Sometimes the bombs make the houses shake a little. They make holes in the roof. Nothing will fall on you there.

Margaret Except the piano. (*Pause. Quietly.*) Gillian's Mother and Father sleep in one bed, not two.

Doris Are you getting into bed? (*Rhetorical:* **Margaret** *isn't.*)

Margaret Yes. (*Lights fade from here on.* **Margaret** *gets into bed.*) Suky – ! (*She holds the doll tight.*)

Doris Tuck you up . . . tuck you in.

Margaret Will Father Christmas know I'm under the piano?

Doris I expect so – see Margaret, you're a parcel and I'm wrapping you up!

Margaret *And* they've got a Christmas tree. Why can't *we* have a tree with candles? Can't we?

Doris *Mayn't* we.

Margaret Mayn't we.

Doris No. Pine needles cause a mess. Besides, candles are dangerous.

Margaret Can Hitler see them?

Doris You never know.

Margaret (*impressed*) Does Hitler fly over our house?

Doris Have you said your prayers? (*Lights very dim now.*)

Margaret No.

Doris I'll say night-night then. (*Going.*)

Margaret Stay a minute! (**Doris** *pauses.* **Margaret** *doesn't know how to keep her.*) Do you and Father say your prayers? (*Pause.*) Do you?

Doris Father does. I think that does very nicely for the both of us.

Margaret Do *you*?

Doris I'm saying goodnight now.

Margaret Will we win the war?

Doris Not if you don't keep quiet and go to sleep. (**Doris** *goes to the door.*)

Margaret What do you mean? (*Pause.*) Gillian says, in parts of Manchester there's nothing left, just bricks squashed. She says people get squashed under there. (*Silence.*) Mother? . . .

Doris Father will be home soon.

Margaret (*calls*) Mother – (*Pause.*) Mummy . . . (*Pause.*) What happens when you die?

Doris (*long pause*) I'll bring you some cocoa presently. (*She goes.*)

The sound of aircraft.

Margaret Sssh Suky Ssh! – No, I won't hold you. You ought to go to sleep now, by yourself. You don't need your Mummy to·kiss you. You're eight years old.

Lights black out. **Margaret** *exits taking the bedding with her.* **Jackie** *takes her place under the piano.* **Doris** *returns, with a floral overall over her clothes. Lights up bright. Birdsong. A May day, it is 1961.* **Doris** *is 61,* **Jackie** *is 9.*

Doris Jackie? (*Peers under the piano.*) Jackie! What *are* you doing under the piano?

Jackie Seeing what it's like. Mummy says you used to put her to bed under the piano here in the Second World War. And listen to the wireless . . .

Doris Margaret says you read a lot of books.

Jackie Only 'cos she won't let me watch telly. Daddy does. Why d'you call her Margaret?

Doris Because she's *my* little girl. You are always your Mother's child, my Mother used to say.

Jackie She's my Mummy.

Doris I'm her Mummy.

Jackie Yes but she calls you 'Mother'. That's different.

Doris How?

Jackie Just is. (*Pause.*) You won't tell Mummy about the cup I broke?

Doris It was only utility.

Jackie What's that?

Doris From the war. (*Pause.*) I'll tell her . . . you've been a very good girl. All by yourself, too. (*Pause.*) We'll go in the garden and break two jam jars presently.

Jackie Why?

Doris Everything goes in threes. If you break one thing, more is sure to follow.

Jackie Is that true?

Doris So they say.

Jackie Who's they? (*She strokes the piano.*) Why has your bath got feet? This is very old wood.

Doris As old as your grandparents. It's the first thing we bought after we got married.

Jackie Yes it is a bit old fashioned.

Doris (*rubs wood*) Classical.

Jackie (*strokes the white flowers in the vase on the piano*) Are these plastic?

Doris No! *Wax.*

Jackie Can't you afford plastic?

Doris I've had those *years.* Since your mother was a little girl.

Jackie We've got new kitchen chairs with yellow seats.

Doris Yes. Your Mother likes all these new formicas, doesn't she. (*Disapproving.*)

Jackie When you spill your lunch you can wipe it off straight away. *All* our furniture's new. Poor old Gran. It's all old here, isn't it?

Doris It was new once. (*Pause.* **Jackie** *contemplates this.*)

Jackie Do you know something?

Doris What?

Jackie I like your old house.

Doris (*pleased*) You tell your Mother.

Jackie Why?

Doris Do it for me.

Jackie (*musing*) We don't have a larder you can hide in, either.

Doris We'll make fairy cakes, then we can give Margaret tea when she arrives. (*Pause.*)

Margaret. Act One, Scene Two, Royal Court Theatre

Doris and Rosie meet in the wasteground as children.

Act One, Scene Three, Contact Theatre

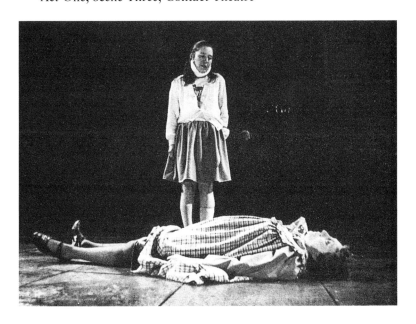

Margaret comes to Manchester to take Jackie's baby, Rosie.
Act One, Scene Six, Contact Theatre

The day Margaret leaves home she tells her mother she will
never have children. Act One, Scene Seven, Contact Theatre

Rosie, Margaret and Jackie on Rosie's eighth birthday, in Margaret and Ken's garden. Act One, Scene Ten, Royal Court Theatre

Doris, Margaret, Rosie and Jackie, clearing Jack's house
after his death. Act Two, Contact Theatre

Margaret and Doris, as above. Act Two, Contact Theatre

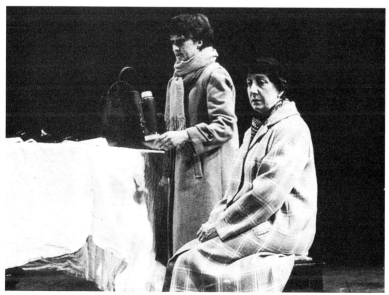

Photo: John Haynes

Margaret tells her mother that her husband has left her.
Act Three, Scene One, Contact Theatre

Jackie and Rosie in Margaret's office.
Act Three, Scene Two, Royal Court Theatre

Rosie has found her birth certificate and discovered Jackie is her
real mother. Act Three, Scene Five, Contact Theatre

Rosie and Doris. Rosie solves the solitaire on her sixteenth birthday.
Act Three, Scene Seven, Contact Theatre

Doris on the day of her engagement to Jack, beside Rosie
playing solitaire. Act Three, Scene Eight, Contact Theatre

Jackie Lucy Parker in my class can do the hoola hoop to a hundred.

Doris And later on I'll teach you how to say grace, in French.

Jackie What for?

Doris (*holds out her hand*) Come along, let's go and find Mrs Beeton.

Jackie *hugs* **Doris**. **Doris** *hesitates for a second, then bends and embraces* **Jackie**.

Doris Kiss your old Granny, then.

Jackie (*kisses* **Doris**. **Doris** *kisses* **Jackie**) It's much nicer here.

They go off together.

Lights dim again. **Doris** *re-enters, without her overall, dressed as at the beginning of the scene.* **Margaret** *is not there, but the doll lies a little way from the piano.* **Doris** *carries a utility ware mug.*

Doris Margaret? I brought you some cocoa. (*Sound of planes, distant.*) Margaret? Are you alseep? . . . Dear? (*Silence.*) Well then. You'll just have to drink it cold in the morning. (*She sees the doll and picks it up. Going.*) Can't waste good sugar and cocoa. (*Goes.*)

Scene Three

The Wasteground. A secret place which only girls can get to. Two cats wail like babies. **Rosie** *runs in. She finds the bits of sweet wrapper from the voodoo in Scene One. Arranges them in the pattern which* **Jackie** *used. Looks at them for a moment. Picks them up. Scatters the pieces, watches them fall.* **Doris** *runs in.*

Rosie Mum's got the curse. (*Pause.*) Maybe we did it!

Doris (*pause*) What curse?

Rosie *The* curse.

Doris Oh. Yes . . . How d'you know she's got it?

Rosie You can tell.

Doris How?

Rosie Just can. Mum's been cross with me all morning.

Doris Well?

Rosie Well you'd be cross if you'd been cursed. (*Pause.*) Like in that story. She might turn into something.

Doris Will she die?

Rosie You have the curse until you're an old, old lady.

Doris Then what?

Rosie Then it stops. (*Pause.*) *Then* you die.

Doris Did she prick her finger and bleed?

Rosie Dunno. She might've, but I didn't see any blood.

Doris Cross your heart she's got the curse?

Rosie And hope to die. (*Lowers her voice, conspiratorial.*) We were in the A.B.C. having buns. Mum said she was going to the Ladies. When she came back, she said, 'We'd better go quickly, I've got the curse'. (*Pause.*) So I went into the Ladies to have a look . . . and, sure enough, on the wall, there it was!

Doris (*frightened*) What?

Rosie The little heart-shaped drawing!!

Stunned silence.

Doris Oooh . . .

Rosie I thought she'd been looking different. Sort of oldish in her face.

They savour the moment. Then, fast.

Rosie ⎫
Doris ⎭ Doctors and nurses!.

Doris Bags be nurse!

Rosie I'll be doctor. (*Pause.*) Who'll be patient?

Doris All right. I'll be patient and you be doctor and then it's my turn.

Rosie I've brought our kit.

Rosie *opens a plastic carrier with rattling objects inside it.* **Rosie** *takes out a large sanitary towel and fits it over her head, with the loops over her ears.*

Rosie Good morning Mrs Bradley what seems to be the trouble can you take your knickers off please.

Doris I don't think we ought.

Rosie You been telling?

Doris (*pause*) No.

Rosie You have.

Doris I think Mam knows. What we do . . .

Rosie How, dummy?

Doris (*pause*) She says she can see inside my head.

Rosie We'll just have to pretend, then. (*Coughs.*) Can you lie down please not very nice for the time of year is it.

Doris *hesitates, lies down.*

Rosie Tut tut tut.

Doris Is it very bad?

Rosie I'll just have to feel it.

Doris (*jumps up*) Don't touch.

Rosie But you like it.

Doris I might catch a babby.

Rosie I think you've got one already.

Doris That's my husband's fault, you can't trust him.

Rosie How is your husband?

Doris Oh he's upped and gone.

Rosie Oh I am sorry.

Doris I'm not. You must drop by for a cuppa. That's enough now, your turn.

They swap positions: **Doris** *wears the sanitary towel,* **Rosie** *lies down.*

Rosie Will you have to stethoscope me?

Doris Oh yes all right. (*Takes a kitchen funnel from the carrier bag and listens to* **Rosie**'s *stomach.*)

Rosie Can you hear anything?

Doris Yes I think the babby's coming out.

Rosie Shall I tell my husband?

Doris No not yet. There's no cause for alarm.

Rosie Will it hurt?

Doris PUSH! It's like doing a big poo. Then the babby pops out.

Rosie You know the yellow nightie we hid? Mum wore that when I was born. It's got a dark red stain on it.

Doris It's not, it's brown.

Rosie Blood dries up. When it's very old.

Doris Truly? Let's go and look.

Rosie When a baby's born they cut the cord.

Doris What's that?

Rosie It joins the baby to its mummy.

Doris (*contemplates*) Let's be babbies tomorrow.

Rosie No, it's weddings tomorrow.

Doris Why?

Rosie You have to get married first.

Scene Four

Raynes Park, London, May 1969. The garden of **Ken** *and* **Margaret**'s *suburban semi.* **Jackie** *is nearly 18, wears flared jeans with sewn-on badges;* **Margaret** *is 38, wears a flowered apron and carries a tea towel.* **Jackie** *has her red transistor which blares, 'All*

*You Need is Love'. She sprawls on the grass beside the cherry tree,
next to the swing.* **Margaret** *follows, flustered.*

Margaret (*switches off the transistor*) I should never have let you
go to that party in Hammersmith!

Jackie Please, Mummy, leave me alone.

Margaret You said you were staying with his parents!

Jackie We were. But they didn't mind us sleeping together. Not
everyone has your hang ups.

Margaret Oh you can wound me sometimes, Jackie!

Jackie You sound like Granny now.

Margaret What am I going to tell Daddy?

Jackie If you want me to behave like an adult, then stop treating
me like a child!

Margaret (*pause*) You don't know what might happen.

Jackie I might fall in love.

Margaret (*trying to ignore this*) You can get pregnant the first time,
you know.

Jackie Thanks for telling me now.

Margaret Well if you'd come to me and said –

Jackie Well I did say I wanted to have a talk with you, actually,
and you said 'Tell me while we go round the garden centre', don't
you remember? (*Slight pause.*) Anyway, you can't scare me,
because I'm on the pill, OK?

Margaret Since when?

Jackie Since before Neil and I went away at half term. You knew
that because you've been reading my diary.

Margaret (*momentarily caught*) Well I've no idea, you might be on
drugs, anything! (*Collects herself.*) I know I'm going to sound like
an old fuddy duddy. . . . but . . . (*Stuck.*) It's a serious step you've
taken, you've no idea –

Jackie It was no big deal. It was a relief to get it over with. I cried afterwards. Then I laughed. I expect it's better with someone you're in love with.

Margaret You could have waited.

Jackie Why?

Margaret I had to.

Jackie That's it, isn't it? (*Gets up and goes to the house.*)

Margaret If this affects your A-levels!

Jackie (*stops*) What?

Silence. **Margaret** *has nothing to say.*

Jackie I'm going to make a phone call. Phone Neil. (*Goes into the house.*)

Margaret (*pause. Picks up* Jackie's *transistor*) I had an admirer. He took me to dinner. I'd never eaten oysters before. – Wouldn't let me see the bill, that sort of man. I was sure Ken could tell, when I got in. I'd had my hair done, on a Wednesday. (*Pause.*) Ten years ago.

Blackout.

Scene Five

Cheadle Hulme, Manchester, 1961 as in Scene Two. **Jackie** *is 9,* **Margaret** *is 30,* **Doris** *is 61. The garden. Sound of lawnmower off right.*

Doris *enters with a chair and a rug, and arranges them on the grass. She glares, off right.*

Doris (*calls to right*) Jack! JACK!

The lawnmower sound stops.

Doris Are you coming to have tea with us? Ken and Margaret can't stop long.

Pause. The lawnmower sound starts up again. She shouts.

Well you'd better do round the front, I don't want grass clippings in our tea. (*As the lawnmower fades away to right.*) And mind my lily of the valley! (*She goes back to the house for the tea tray.*)

Enter Jackie *leading* Margaret *by the hand, followed by* Doris.

Jackie And I've been doing the pear tree. Look. (*She shows* Margaret *the painting.*)

Margaret Oh that's lovely darling!

Jackie Grandad let me use his real paints.

Doris He's been teaching you, hasn't he.

Jackie Did you know shadows are purple?

Doris Have you said hello properly?

Jackie (*hugs* Margaret) Are you better?

Margaret Better? (*Looks at* Doris.) Mother . . .

Jackie Where's Daddy?

Margaret He's gone to fill up the car with petrol.

Doris That chair's for you.

Margaret No, really.

Doris The rug will do quite nicely for me. (*Sits.*) Sit down and have some tea.

Margaret Oh we mustn't, I said to Ken we'd be ready to leave as soon as he comes back.

Doris Her bag is packed and in the hall.

Margaret If we stay for tea we won't get home to London till way past Jackie's bedtime.

Jackie I don't mind.

Doris Jackie made the cakes. Didn't you dear?

Pause. Margaret *gives in to pressure and sits.*

Margaret All right Mother. And what have you been doing, darling?

Jackie I broke a cup and then we broke two jam jars.

Margaret Oh dear.

Doris Jackie's been an angel.

Jackie (*offering the cake*) Have the yellow one with the smartie.

Doris I hope you've been taking the iron tablets, dear.

Margaret (*resists temptation to answer back. To* **Jackie**, *for the cake*) Thank you.

Jackie (*says grace in French, very fast*) Que Dieu benisse nôtre pain quotidien. Amen. (*Pause.*)

Margaret Well this is very nice.

Doris And how was Windermere? Did you drive about much?

Margaret We stayed in a lovely guest house, a bit pricey but Ken insisted I was pampered.

Jackie What's pampered?

Doris Nursed.

Pause. **Jackie** *looks at* **Margaret.** **Margaret** *looks at* **Doris.**

Margaret No, pampered is – being spoiled a bit – like you've been, here!

Doris Thank you, Margaret.

Margaret And I brought you some Kendal mint cake! (*Gives it to* **Jackie.**)

Jackie And some for Granny? Never mind Granny, we can share this. (*Breaks it in half and gives half to* **Doris**, *then goes back to her painting.*)

Doris I hope you didn't do too much walking.

Margaret It rained a lot. Luckily there was a nice lounge with a fire. Time to sit and think. You know, Mother, I thought I didn't want it, till I lost it. (*Pause.*) It's been a blessing, you taking Jackie for the week. But I missed you, darling!

Jackie (*goes and hugs* **Margaret**) I cried the first night, didn't I Granny, then at breakfast Grandad let me have your old napkin ring.

Margaret (*holds her*) Oh Jackie.

Jackie And your doll. It's like a real baby, it's got real curled up toes and fingers. 1 was practising. I bathed it and put it to sleep, and it shut its eyes.

Margaret No! (*Gets up.*)

Jackie Mummy –

Doris Jackie – (*Catches hold of her.*)

Jackie I didn't break her, I didn't break the doll!

Doris (*comforts*) Ssh ssh –

Jackie You're hurting! (*Breaks free and runs off, knocking the paint pot across the painting.*)

Doris If you hadn't been so hasty to get that temping job, you would never have lost the baby.

Margaret (*busying herself with the painting*). It'll dry in the evening sun, it'll be all right.

Doris That's for Jack. He wanted something from his grandchild.

Doris *takes the painting.*

Blackout.

Scene Six

A council flat on the Hulme estate, Manchester, early December 1971. Jackie is 19½, Rosie is 3 months, Margaret is 40. A worn piece of rusty red carpet with ashtrays and mugs strewn on it, also the red transistor from Scene Four, now worn and battered, blares out over Rosie's *crying. A Moses basket of blankets represents* Rosie; *the actress playing* Rosie *can be seen making the sounds of the baby crying. As the lights rise,* Jackie *is packing baby clothes into a holdall.*

Radio (*Manchester DJ*). . . Today's highest temperature is expected to be a cold 3°, so wrap up warm. Most roads in the city have been cleared now, but there's still ice and snow on the Pennines, and the forecast is more snow tonight. Police are asking motorists leaving Manchester on Northbound routes to drive slowly because of black ice. Meanwhile, here's something to remind you of summer days . . . ('*Honky Tonk Woman*'.)

Jackie (*packing hurriedly*) I wanted it to look nice and now it won't all go in!

Rosie *yells.*

Jackie (*hits transistor, which goes off*) Ssh, Rosie, please –

Rosie *yells.*

Jackie Shut up!

Rosie *stops crying abruptly.*

Jackie (*gently*) Ssh, ssh, there now . . . Where do you get the energy from, yelling all night? (*Bends over Moses basket, sings haphazard tune.*) My little rabbit, in your little basket . . .

Rosie *coos.*

Jackie Sleep, beautiful . . . ssh . . .

Rosie *makes a little cry as* Jackie *moves away to pack again.*

Jackie (*bends over* Rosie *again*) Please don't be crying when Mummy and Daddy arrive! – Where's your red sock? (*Picks it up and dangles it over* Rosie, *who quietens during:*) Look, it fell out! Give me a smile – yes! There. I even washed your red sock. Washed everything, don't want Mummy to think – (*Holding back tears.*) I've got to clear up, Rosie. – All these ashtrays, Sandra and

Hugh last night, they never think about you, do they? (*Picks up ashtray.*)

Margaret (*from off*) Hello?

Jackie Oh shit, the mess – Come in!

Margaret (*entering*) Hello Jackie.

Jackie (*immediately casual*) Hi Mummy.

Margaret It's not locked!

Jackie I knew it would be you.

Margaret You've been smoking.

Jackie Journey from London OK?

Margaret Not how I remembered, Mosside. All these tower blocks . . .

Jackie Is Daddy – he's not –

Margaret Waiting in the car.

Jackie He didn't mind? – I'm sorry, I couldn't face –

Margaret He understands.

Pause.

Jackie This is Rosie, Mummy.

Margaret I – came up the stairs. (*Pause.*) Lift is out of order. (*Pause.*) Lot of stairs.

Jackie . . . Please.

Margaret (*long pause*) Three months.

Jackie Say hello.

Margaret (*goes to the Moses basket. Pause*) Pretty.

Jackie (*goes also*) You think so?

Margaret You had curly eyelashes like that.

Jackie (*pleased*) Did I?.

Margaret Hello Rosie . . . (*Kisses her.*)

Jackie Don't wake her!

Margaret Of course not!

Jackie I'm sorry, it's just –

Margaret You think I don't know?

Rosie *coos quietly.*

Margaret (*very tenderly*) Ssh, there now.

Rosie *murmurs.*

Jackie (*turns away*) I've packed her things . . . here. (*Gives* Margaret *the holdall.*) And her bottles are in this carrier. There's a bit of powdered milk left –

Margaret Oh you really don't need –

Jackie Well what would I do with it?

Awkward pause. **Margaret** *looks through the clothes in the holdall.*

Margaret I've been to Mothercare. Got some of those new disposable nappies, like you said. Quite different from when you were a baby. (*Sees another carrier, goes to pick it up.*) What about this bag – what a sweet – won't she want this dress with the rabbit on?

Jackie Leave those! – Things she's grown out of.

Margaret Why did you have to try! All by yourself? Didn't you believe me?

Jackie I wanted to see if our theories worked . . . (*Pause.*) But when I came back from hospital everyone had cleared out. You'd think I had VD, not a new baby.

Margaret He should be here with you, your – (*Stuck for word.*) – Rosie's father. – You in these flats . . .

Jackie (*calm*) Mummy, I told you. He visits; and sends money. It was my decision.

Margaret Yes but you had no idea! I told you, I told you! Nothing, for nearly three months, nothing, since the day she was born, then a phone call, out of the blue, the potatoes boiled dry!

Jackie You knew I'd phone, one day. (*Slight pause.*)

Margaret Look at you now, a year ago you had everything, you were so excited about the art school, new friends, doing so well –

Jackie (*angry*) I'll go back! Yes I will, finish the degree, I won't fail both things! Only think about her at night, her cheek against mine, soft and furry, like an apricot . . .

Rosie *makes a snuffling noise in her sleep.*

Jackie . . . She'll be happy, won't she? . . .

Margaret After you phoned . . . after you asked us . . . Daddy went upstairs and got your old high chair down from the attic. (*Pause.*) Like sisters, he said. A new little sister . . . (*Bends down to* Rosie.) Aren't you, precious?

Jackie (*panics*) Mummy – she's got to know – I can't come and visit, with her not knowing, I can't!

Margaret Jackie, darling, we can't go over this again – you know as well as I do it would be impossible –

Jackie I don't believe you!

Margaret When she's grown up, you can tell her; when she's sixteen.

Jackie It'll be too late!

Silence.

Give me back the bags.

Margaret (*gently*) You've got such opportunities.

Jackie Expectations.

Margaret Yes!

Jackie Yours.

Margaret You've got to –

Jackie Why? (*Pulls away holdall.*) Why not just Rosie?

Margaret You've got to go further than me – and Rosie too. (*Quietly.*) Otherwise . . . what's it been worth?

Jackie (*pause*) Here, take them. (*Gives* **Margaret** *the bags.*) You haven't told Granny and Grandad?

Margaret Not yet. I'll talk to them. (*Tentative.*) – Perhaps you could stay with them, just till Christmas, while you find a new flat? . . . (*Bends to* **Rosie.**) My little lamb . . . What's this?

Jackie She has to have a red sock to go to sleep.

Margaret You keep one.

Jackie (*puts one sock in her pocket*) Love her for me . . .

Margaret *picks up the Moses basket.*

Jackie I'll help you to the car.

Margaret It's all right, Daddy will be there. (**Margaret** *picks up the bags. As she goes to the door.*)

Jackie I'll come for Christmas. And visit, lots. (*Pause.*) Whenever I can afford the fare to London.

Margaret *exits.*

Jackie (*calls after them*) Sing to her at bathtime, especially the rabbit song . . . (*Silence. Pause. She picks up the bag she told* **Margaret** *to leave. As she pulls out the clothes, she is suddenly hysterically happy. She holds up the rabbit dress.*) – Wore this the day you first smiled, you wouldn't let go of my hair, – do you remember?! (*Holds up another.*) – And your first bonnet . . . (*Gentle.*) And the shawl . . . wrapped you up, like a parcel, the day we left hospital; all the way back in a taxi, bringing you home . . . (*Pause.*) Our secrets, Rosie. I'll take care of them. (*Pause.*) You'll never call me 'Mummy'. (*Silence. Screams.*) Rosie! Come back! – Mummy, Mummy!

Blackout. For a moment in the darkness, the sound of a baby crying. In a dim light we see **Margaret** *rocking a bundle. She*

*comforts the baby with the following words, until the baby
quietens and coos:*

Margaret There now, there now, hush! Did you have a nasty
dream? My precious. Mummy's here now. Mummy's here, Rosie.
There now . . . Did you have a bad dream, Jackie? It's all right. Ssh
. . . ssh . . .

As the lights come up bright for the next scene, **Margaret** *turns and
billows out the sheet which was forming the bundle.*

Scene Seven

*Cheadle Hulme, Manchester, 1951. A hot August day. A distant
rumble of thunder.* **Doris** *wearing a sensible beige skirt, and*
Margaret, *wearing ski pants, are in the garden folding a single bed
sheet. One more sheet remains on the line and one of* **Jack's** *shirts.
Socks lie on the grass, one maroon one a little way off. The rest of
the washing is already folded and in a washing basket.* **Doris** *is 51
and* **Margaret** *is 20.*

Doris I'll be glad when they put an end to clothes rationing. These
sheets are quite threadbare in the middle.

Sound of light aircraft going overhead.

Doris (*studies the sky*) R.A.F. from the base at Padgate.

Margaret They're B29s, not Lancasters!

Doris I'll be glad when they're gone. (*Disdain.*) Americans.

Margaret Mother! Without them we couldn't have won the –

Doris Are you going to help me fold this sheet, or are you just
going to stand there all afternoon identifying aircraft!

Margaret (*staring at the sky*) Maybe one of them's Ken.

Doris (*they hold the sheet by the corners and tug*) I don't see how
it can be, if he's calling in half an hour.

They shake the sheet vigorously.

Margaret I can't wait to live in London! (*No reply.*) Ken says he can get a job there. He's frightfully clever.

They balloon the sheet up into the air.

Margaret I'm in love, Mother.

Distant rumble of thunder. **Doris** *looks up at the sky.*

Doris It's not going to hold. (*Pause.*)

They pull diagonals to stretch the sheet.

Margaret And I'm going to learn to type! Ken says it will be helpful if we need a second income. (*As they shake the sheet.*) Typing's far more useful than all those stupid school certificates. I'll get a *proper* job.

Doris What do you call running a home? (*Looks up at the sky.*) I knew we were in for a storm.

Margaret I'm not wasting my life.

Doris (*angry*) Thank you Margaret! (*They fold the sheet lengthwise.*) Pull! (**Margaret** *pulls so hard that* **Doris** *lets go and they jerk back from each other.*)

Doris There's no need to snatch it out of my hands! There see, now you've spoiled it all.

Margaret Well you can pick it up again, can't you! (*Pause.* **Doris** *picks it up, they resume folding.*) I'm not going to have a family, babies and all that. Ken and I have decided.

Doris (*distant rumble of thunder*) It will break, soon.

They fold the sheet lengthwise.

And what makes you so sure you can keep Mother Nature at bay?

They close in chest to chest and **Margaret** *gives her corners to* **Doris**, *who folds the sheet in half and half again during.*

Margaret (*grandly*) There's THINGS you can get . . . I've heard about them.

Doris I'm not talking about that. (*Cradles folded sheet.*) I'm talking about the *desire* . . . for little arms reaching up and clinging round your neck. (*She buries her face in the sheet, then holds it out to* **Margaret** *to do likewise.*) Smell: lavender. From the beds, there. Mother Nature is very hard to fight. It's not just a question of rubber things or what have you.

Margaret 'Little arms clinging' . . . There, see, that's what I don't want. That's the difference between our generations. Mother.

Doris Well I'm glad to know you've worked it out, Margaret. Can you sort out Father's socks, please?

Margaret (*picking the socks off the grass and pairing them*) You want a nice snapshot for the family album don't you? Proof, to show the neighbours. Well I'm going to be different! Women did so much during the war: there's nothing to stop us now.

Doris Ha!

Margaret You think I'm being selfish, don't you?

Doris I felt a few drops, then. (*Pause.*) What makes you think I wanted children?

Margaret Mother!

Doris I had a job once too. I know it was only teaching, but . . . (*Pause. To stop herself.*) there's an odd maroon one over there, on the grass. (*Pause. Warning* **Margaret**.) Of course, Father has absolutely no idea. One would never . . . tell him. (*Pause.*) There wasn't any choice, then; so I don't know whether it was my need – to love him, if you know what I mean . . . or his desire – for a son. (*Long pause.* **Doris** *bends and picks up a sock.*) Horrible colours he likes. Not my choice, maroon . . . Not my choice at all . . . (*Pause.*)

Margaret The garden is always so lovely, Mother. May I take a cutting, off one of your geraniums, to London with me?

Doris Oh Margaret . . . why does it have to be London? (*Sound of raucous car horn, which repeats.*) Oh I do wish people wouldn't do that! Brings down the tone of the neighbourhood!

Margaret It's Ken! He's bought an Austin Healey – it's got a folding roof – you must come and see! I said to honk and I'd move

Father's car into the garage so Ken can back into the drive – I'll
have a lot of cases to load into the boot.

Doris That nice Graham next door. All those trips he took you on,
to the ornamental gardens at Bellevue.

Margaret Yes, Mother. Well I'm *not* going to be a Manchester
dentist's wife.

Doris I must say, Jack asked my mother before there was any talk
of weddings.

Margaret Have you still got your posy?

Doris He's reversing straight into my lily of the valley!

Margaret He's not.

Doris He is.

Margaret He's not, just parking.

Doris Curious method of parking.

Margaret That's typical, you think all Americans are brash and
wear loud check shirts and chew gum and want to marry English
girls. You're just prej– . . .

Doris Margaret, that's enough! (*Pause.*) After all, he is going to
marry an English girl.

Margaret Oh Mother, don't look at me like that with your lips
pressed together.

Margaret *exits.*

Doris *folds the remaining sheet and puts it in the basket during this
speech:*

Doris Well it's too late now. These sheets are damp. I knew this
lovely summer wouldn't last. (*Pause.*) I suppose I should get the
best service out, for tea. (*Rumble of thunder, close.*) She'll need bed
linen. These are all worn out . . . Something old, something new.
So they say.

Doris *picks up the basket of washing and starts towards the house.*
Crack of thunder overhead. Doris *drops the basket, which spills*
everywhere. Immediately, the sound of pouring rain on leaves.
Doris *stands and contemplates the spoiled washing all around her*
as the pouring rain grows louder. Lights fade slowly to blackout.

Scene Eight

The Wasteground. Rosie *skipping, chants.*

Rosie Georgie, Porgie pudding and pie,
Kiss the girls and make them cry,
When the girls come out to play –

Jackie (*runs up, one hand behind her back.* Rosie *stops.*) I went to
the boys' den.

Rosie You said you wouldn't!

Jackie Only slightly.

Rosie You're out of the gang.

Jackie I got the penknife back.

Rosie I don't believe you.

Jackie (*takes the penknife from behind her back and holds it out*
between them) So there.

Rosie So what.

Jackie I kissed a boy.

Rosie You didn't!

Jackie I did.

Rosie What's it like?

Jackie I think I'm in love.

Rosie How d'you know?

Jackie Because this boy made me cry. Daddy makes Mummy cry and she says it's because she loves him. (*Opens penknife blade.*) Now we can do the Vow.

Rosie (*backing away*) It's too late. You've probably got his seed now and it'll grow and grow and fill you up.

Jackie You're still my best friend.

Rosie Don't talk to me about best friends because I'm never playing with you again.

Jackie (*pause*) Kissing wasn't as good as best friends.

Rosie Why d'you do it then?

Jackie To get the penknife.

Rosie (*pause*) You didn't need to kiss a boy. You could have given him some bubble gum.

Jackie I did. He wanted a kiss as well. (*Pause.* **Jackie** *holds the blade up.*) They said I'm a cissy.

Rosie You are.

Jackie (*holds up index finger and ceremoniously jabs the tip with the penknife. Studies it*) I'm bleeding.

Rosie Do I do it too?

Jackie Yes.

Rosie (*takes the knife and stabs her own index finger*) Ready.

They face each other and hold fingertips together and recite.

Rosie ⎱Truth is honesty
Jackie ⎰Honesty is true,
        Keep your promise
        And I'll keep you.

They step back and suck their fingers, **Jackie** *puts the penknife away.*

Rosie You can't ever lie to me now. (*Pause.*) Can you see into the future?

Jackie (*frightened*) A bit.

Rosie Will you have a look for me?

Jackie (*pause*) It'll happen anyway. Mummy says don't cross bridges.

Rosie Is that a spell?

Jackie I don't know. She just says it.

Rosie At night?

Jackie I heard her say it to Daddy, in the garage.

Pause, they look at each other.

Rosie ⎱
Jackie ⎰ Don't-cross-bridges!

Rosie It must be a spell.

Blackout.

Scene Nine

Telephone conversation, early December 1971, later on the same day as Scene Six.

Margaret *in Raynes Park, London, aged 40.* **Doris** *in Cheadle Hulme, aged 71.* **Margaret** *dressed as for Scene Six, with the Moses basket beside her.*

Doris Hello?

Margaret Hello?

Doris Margaret?

Margaret Mother? Oh, I was just about to ring you. It's not gone six has it?

Doris Two minutes ago. We've just got the news on.

Margaret Oh dear . . . I'm sorry, I was just seeing to . . . (*Distant* Rosie *cries.*) . . . to Ken.

Doris Is he poorly again?

Margaret Oh, no, no! Well, a slight cold. Very slight.

Doris *You* don't sound too well.

Margaret I'm fine.

Doris You don't look after yourself, dear.

Margaret (*pause*) Mother, why did you ring?

Doris Oh, just to see if you were all right . . .

Margaret How did you know?

Doris (*matter of fact*) What, dear?

At the same time Rosie *cries in the distance again.* Margaret *puts her hand over the receiver and collects herself.*

Margaret How's Father?

Doris (*pause*) We've still not seen Jackie.

Margaret She's been . . . since when?

Doris Well it's been a year, now.

Margaret I've only seen her – slightly . . .

Doris I suppose she's busy with her studies.

Margaret Oh yes, very.

Doris Only your Father and I thought she might visit, being in Manchester herself now. She's not moved?

Margaret Well, yes, I'm not sure . . .

Doris It was Jack's birthday last week.

Margaret Didn't you get the cards?

Doris Yes, very nice. (*Pause.*) But he usually gets a hand-painted one from Jackie.

Margaret Well . . . you know how it is, she's got to rebel while she's still a teenager.

Doris What?

Margaret Revise. She's got to revise, for her exams.

Doris We thought we might go and visit her.

Margaret Oh no! I shouldn't . . . just yet. She's decorating, decorating her new flat.

Doris She should have asked us. I've plenty of furnishings put by that I don't need any more.

Margaret How's Father?

Doris Oh, creeping, creeping. Can't do anything with his hands now of course. A mither he was in, trying to sign the will.

Margaret You said.

Doris So I sold his painting things. Some of those easels he's had since we were first married.

Margaret Mother! Why didn't you tell me? Not the sable brushes?

Doris (*pause*) No. Jack wants Jackie to have them. (*Pause.*) Of course I said to him I don't suppose she'll want those, being at a Polytechnic. (*Pause.*) He sets great store by her, you know.

Margaret I'd like you to come and visit us.

Doris We're coming at Christmas. Or don't you want us this year?

Margaret Of course Mother! I thought perhaps the week after next . . .

Doris What is it?

Margaret I can't explain on the phone.

Doris You're not hiding anything from us?

Margaret No!

Doris Good or bad dear?

Margaret What? Oh. (*Long pause.*) Good. (**Rosie** *cries, distant.*)
Very.

Doris It's not that sofa you were telling us about?

Margaret No, it's . . .

Doris Well that's two minutes dear. I'll finish now.

Margaret Yes.

Doris Father will be so pleased to know . . .

Margaret What?

Doris About Jackie.

Margaret What?!

Doris Revising for her exams. I'm saying goodnight now.

Margaret Goodnight. (*The line has already gone dead.*) Jackie,
what are you doing to me . . . ?

Blackout on **Margaret** *and* **Doris.**

Scene Ten

Raynes Park, London, September 1979. The garden of **Ken** *and*
Margaret's *home. Distant jingle of icecream van.* **Rosie** *is 8.* **Jackie**
is 27, **Margaret** *is 48. The cherry tree has grown, the swing is as in
Scene Four. It is* **Rosie**'s *eighth birthday. Enter* **Rosie,** *carrying an
old spoon and* **Margaret**'s *doll Suky from Scene Two. It is a baby
doll, now bald except for a few tufts which have been spiked.*

Rosie It's my birthday today and it's all gone wrong already. I'm
going to bury you, Suky. Eight is too old for dolls. I want a Sex
Pistols tee shirt. Some hope. Unless Jackie brings me one! I'd have
buried you ages and ages ago, Suky, if you hadn't been Mum's. I
couldn't care less now if Mum sees me doing this. (*Digs in the
tub.*) Suky. Stupid name. Even cutting your hair off it won't go
punk. I bet Mum cuddled you and stuff, didn't she? Well I only
hug people when I want to, not when it's visitors. (*Holds doll over
her face. Pause.*) When I want to I can hug harder than anyone. In
the world. (*Pause.*) I'm saving it. (*Pause. Digs hole. Lowers the*

doll over it, then holds it closer to her.) I was going to give you away to the Toy Collection at School, d'you know that? Mummies give their babies away sometimes. They do. (*Pause. Slowly lays the doll in the hole.*) Shut up crying. There, see, I'm putting you in this urn. People get buried in urns. (*Covering the doll over with earth.*) Jackie'll be here soon. She never cries. No one else at school has a sister who's a grown-up. I might easily run away with Jackie and live with her. Then you'd be sorry, Suky. So would Mum. (*Suddenly bright, as if enormously relieved.*) I'm going to paint the cherry tree now – for Jackie.

Rosie *lies on the grass painting.* **Jackie** *enters with a very lavish birthday cake and candles.*

Jackie Happy-birthday-to-you! . . . Rosie?

Rosie Why did you buy me one? Mum usually makes me one.

Jackie Thanks.

Rosie I mean, it doesn't look as good as this. And she always makes chocolate because she thinks I like it.

Jackie Why don't you tell her you don't?

Rosie Oh you know Mum. Never listens. I think she just likes making birthday cakes. Even *Dad* gets one!

Jackie Let's light the candles.

Rosie Shouldn't we wait for Mum?

Jackie Oh, yes.

Rosie (*pause*) Has it got drink in it?

Jackie Rum. A bit.

Rosie Mum and Dad never drink anything exciting. You know that funny shaped bottle you brought them from Mexico? It's still in the cabinet.

Jackie Well I brought Mum some Greek lace this time. Sort of thing she wouldn't treat herself to.

Rosie She's so *mean*! D'you know, she wouldn't even buy me a Sex Pistols tee shirt, she says 'No dear, you haven't grown out of last year's summer dresses'. As if I could be seen wearing those!

Margaret (*enters with a tray*) What's that dear? Here we are, celebration drinks! How long is it since you were last here, Jackie?

Jackie (*silence*) I don't know. Shall we light the candles Rosie?

Rosie Can I?! (*As they light the candles.*) One . . . year . . . and four months.

Margaret I thought we'd have some of the tequila you brought us, Jackie. We keep it for special occasions.

Jackie (*to* **Rosie**) See.

Rosie Me too?

Margaret A little bit.

Pause. All three watch the candles burn.

Margaret Magic.

Jackie I used to wish . . .

Margaret (*cuts in*) Blow the candles out.

Rosie I think Jackie wants . . .

Margaret Now darling, before it spoils.

A moment while **Rosie** *hesitates.*

Margaret Blow the candles out.

Rosie (*blows the candles out*) Done it! (*Pause.*)

Jackie Wish, Rosie!

Margaret No, you hold the knife and wish as you cut it . . .

Jackie No, you wish *first*!

Margaret No, Rosie and I always . . .

Rosie Oh stop it, you two!

Margaret Don't we, Rosie. (*Silence.*) *I'll* cut it then. It must have cost Jackie a lot.

Rosie I don't want any now. (*Gets up.*)

Jackie Don't go. What's this, Rosie love?

Rosie You mustn't look! I can't paint like you can!

Jackie It's lovely, Rosie.

Rosie 'S not, the sun's running down into the grass.

Jackie It could be abstract, all swirls.

Rosie Don't be stupid! It's a mess, even you can see that.

Jackie Can I keep it?

Rosie (*snatches it away*) It's for Mum. Here, Mum. (*Gives it to her.*) It's gone wrong.

Margaret It's lovely! Thank you, pet. (*She and* **Rosie** *embrace.*) Say sorry to Jackie.

Rosie Sorry, Jackie.

Jackie *is watching intently.*

Margaret (*looks at the painting*) Where shall we put it? The kitchen walls are choc-a-bloc.

Rosie On the fridge.

Margaret (*laughs*) Run and put it there, before someone sits on it, like Daddy did.

Rosie *exits. Awkward pause.*

Margaret How's Manchester?

Jackie Fine.

Margaret Working hard?

Jackie Yes. (*Uneasy silence.*)

Margaret I've got a full-time job now, too.

Jackie (*pleased*) That's good. I'm hoping to open a gallery of my own in a couple of years, with Simon, if we can get the backing.

Margaret Oh I did like Simon.

Jackie We're not – together any more.

Margaret (*gently*) It would be nice, Jackie, if you found someone, I know you'll hate me for saying this, but it could be very lonely when you're –

Jackie Mummy – (*Stops.*) Simon wanted children, I tried to believe I could start again. – Stupid – I just kept dreaming about Rosie.

Moment.

Rosie (*calls*) Mum! – Where's the Blu-tac?

Margaret (*calls*) In the cupboard with the carrier bags.

Rosie (*calls*) Oh, s' all right . . .

Jackie She doesn't need me, does she?

Margaret No.

Rosie (*running in*) No what?

Jackie No you don't ride your bike on the main road.

Rosie I do! Me and Zoe Taylor nearly crashed, we were kazooming –

Jackie Well you shouldn't! NEVER, ever – I'm sorry Rosie, I didn't mean to shout at you – (**Rosie** *has run off. Silence.*) I do worry about her getting run over, or getting ill, or lost or attacked, and me not being there . . .

Margaret I worry about YOU.

Jackie Still?

Margaret Mothers don't grow out of it.

Jackie (*hands* **Margaret** *a small carefully wrapped package*) Here.

Margaret A present – for me? (*Opens it.*)

Jackie It's lace.

Margaret (*turning it over in her hands*) Where was it you were this time? – Greece? (*Bemused.*) I try to imagine what it's like, when you go off on these trips by yourself, no one else to think about!

Jackie It's from the convent on the island. The nuns have used the same pattern for a thousand years.

Margaret Thank you dear.

Jackie (*slight pause*) Mummy, I've been given a rise; new bikes are expensive . . . I want to give you a cheque –

Margaret How dare you! This isn't one of your art deals! (*Snatches the cheque and tears it up.*)

Rosie (*runs in*) What is it Mum? (*Hugs Margaret. To Jackie.*) I hate you! (*Clings to Margaret.*) Mum, I want you to see where I've put my painting.

Margaret (*as they go into the house together*) . . . All right darling.

Jackie *stays sitting a moment. She sees the old spoon and scattered earth, then goes to the cherry tree in its tub, digs out the doll which* **Rosie** *buried, brushes it down. It is naked except for one red sock.* **Jackie** *takes the other red sock from her pocket. As she puts the sock on the doll the lights fade to blackout, so that as she raises the doll to her cheek she is only just visible.*

Blackout.

Act Two

Cheadle Hulme, Manchester, December 1982. The large front room of Doris and Jack's house. A French window to the garden and a door to the hall. Dustsheets over boxes and the piano. Snow on a rose bush outside the window. Doris is 82, Margaret is 51, Jackie is 30, Rosie is 11.

Rosie (*enters with a flashlight, swings it round. Pause*) Grandad? You in here? (*Silence, listens.*) Well if you're listening, I want to tell you that it was pretty stupid, what you did – I mean, leaving the house and stuff to Jackie. Mum and Gran were mega hurt, you know that? (*Pause.*) Grandad . . . ? I'd like to know, did you do it because you like Jackie best . . . or because you're jealous? (*Silence. Listens. A rustle. Rosie jumps, swings the flashlight round.*) Mice. (*Pause.*) I'm not scared of you, Grandad. it's the others who are. You didn't get me. (*Switches off the flashlight and goes out to garden through French windows, shutting them behind her.*)

Enter Jackie carrying boxes and binliners. She puts these down and exits.

Margaret enters with a bag and rubber gloves, guiding Doris.

Doris Two months ago Saturday Jack died, and the house hasn't been aired since.

Margaret Well we can soon put that right, Mother.

Doris I doubt it.

Lights on suddenly and bright. Doris startled.

Jackie (*re-enters*) I turned the power on, and the water.

Doris Oh I don't think that'll be necessary.

Margaret Mother we have to see to clear up.

Jackie You don't have to worry about bills now, Granny, I've worked it all out. (*To Margaret.*) I've backed the van up the drive so we can load things straight in.

Doris My lily of the valley!

Jackie I couldn't see. There's snow over everything.

Doris It was terrible on the motorway driving up.

Jackie Have you had a good time in London?

Doris . . . Terrible . . . (*Still referring to the journey.*)

Margaret Yes well we're here now, Mother. Have some tea, I've brought a flask. (*Gets out the thermos and pours a cup.*)

Doris I'm quite all right. You have some.

Margaret I want to get on.

Jackie Sit down while the house warms up.

Doris I don't want to be a nuisance to anyone.

Margaret (*wavers, cup in hand*) Jackie?

Jackie Got sugar in it?

Margaret Yes.

Jackie You know I don't.

Margaret You've got no sense of compromise, have you?

Rosie *knocks on the French windows with a white rose.*

Margaret Look at Rosie.

Doris She'll catch her death.

Margaret She never does. (*Lets Rosie in.*)

Rosie Look what I found!

Doris Is it wax?

Margaret A Christmas rose.

Doris It's dead.

Jackie It's not, it's frozen.

Rosie That's dead.

Jackie We could unfreeze it.

Rosie Even you can't organise roses to come alive.

Doris (*going to French windows*) They should all have been pruned by now . . . all blown down by the storms.

Rosie C'mon, we can't prune them now.

Doris I don't want whoever buys this house to think Jack and I didn't know about roses.

Jackie We can pay to have the garden done, before we sell.

Doris (*stiff*) All that money, and Jack would never spend a penny of it.

Rosie Mum, can Jackie and I make a snowman?

Margaret Rosie we've only got today and tomorrow to get this house sorted out. I don't suppose Jackie wants us in her flat any longer than that.

Jackie Mummy, you can stay as long as you like, you know that!

Margaret You said you've even been using your bedroom to store paintings.

Jackie That was before the exhibition. Anyway Rosie's room is always ready.

Rosie Mum, can't I stay –

Margaret (*sharp*) Rosie. (*Pause.*) Now Jackie, you tell us all where to start. Seeing as Father left you in charge of everything.

Jackie Come on Mummy, that's only because I live in Manchester too. He knew I'd be on the spot to deal with the house.

Margaret I suppose being born in this house doesn't count, Jackie. (*Beat.*)

Jackie (*passing a binliner to* **Doris**) Granny, you take a binliner and –

Doris She's going to put it all in dustbins!

Jackie You choose which curtains you'd like from this room, the rest we'll leave for the auction.

Margaret I'll make a start on the crockery, then. (*Pulls dustsheet off a set of shelves. A willow pattern service is on the lower shelves, ornaments and framed photographs above.*)

Rosie Okay don't talk to me.

Margaret Rosie, bring that box over and start scrunching up newspaper for packing.

Rosie (*kicking the box over to* **Margaret**) Do some chores instead.

Jackie I'm sure you'll want to keep the willow pattern, won't you Granny?

Doris Old. Cracked.

They wrap and pack the willow pattern during the following dialogue.

Margaret Mother, you sit tight and we'll pass you things to wrap.

Doris I shan't want any of this. Jackie's possessions now, according to the will.

Jackie Granny, you'll need things for the house in Oldham.

Doris It's not a house. It's an end terrace.

Rosie Come off it Gran, that's a bit mean. Jackie bought you exactly the house you wanted.

Margaret Rosie! Don't be rude.

Rosie Well I think you're both being rude to Jackie. She can't help what Grandad did.

Doris It seems that sixty years of housewifery counted for nothing, in Jack's eyes.

Margaret Your house has always been a gleaming example to us, Mother. Rosie, can you fetch some more newspaper please.

Doris Well Jackie didn't follow it, did she. (*Slight pause.*) Jack noticed *her* sort of work, because he was always asking how her painting exhibitions were going. And since Jackie didn't care to visit much, I had to make it up. And as you know, modern art was never my strong point.

Rosie She hardly ever visits us, Gran.

Jackie – I'm always there for your birthdays, Rosie.

Rosie Most of them.

Jackie I try –

Rosie S'okay Jackie, you have to travel lots, and your work's the most important thing, isn't it. (*Pause.*)

Margaret Funny how a job was never a good enough excuse for me. I think Father disapproved of it.

Rosie But your job's only typing, Mum. (*Slight pause.*) Anyway, Jackie's different, she's got no kids. (*Pause. One mug left at the back of the shelf.*)

Rosie What's this vile mug?

Doris That's utility, Rosie. I used to give Margaret cocoa in that.

Margaret I'd forgotten.

Rosie Mum's always giving us cocoa.

Margaret It's funny, Mother, Jackie and Rosie don't even like cocoa.

Doris You only want what you're denied.

Rosie *passes mug to* **Jackie**, *who wraps it.*

Jackie Oh yes – I broke the handle once – see where Grandad glued it?

Margaret I don't remember.

Jackie Oh – you weren't here.

Margaret Why ever not?

Jackie Well it was the summer you – (*Stuck.*) – weren't well.

Margaret (*pause*) I don't remember.

Pause. Jackie *puts the mug in the box which is now full and tapes it closed.*

Jackie There's the willow pattern, Granny.

Doris That was my wedding. Was never the set I wanted.

Pause.

Jackie Rosie, take Granny into the kitchen and see if there's any pans she'd like to take.

Doris What about the bedrooms?

Margaret What about them, Mother?

Doris Well Rosie will need bed linen.

Rosie What for?

Doris You never know.

Rosie I've got a duvet.

Margaret Rosie.

Rosie I have!

Jackie Rosie, why don't you and Granny go upstairs and sort out some sheets.

Doris Come along, princess.

Rosie I'm not a princess. I'm a punk. – We could get in your old wardrobe, Gran.

Doris Why, love?

Rosie Play sardines. Brill. – Come on Gran.

As Rosie *leads* Doris *out of the room.*

Doris I want to know, when did I stop being Granny, and turn into Gran?

Rosie You like it.

Pause.

Jackie I thought we might have a chat.

Margaret We can while we finish these shelves, can't we.

Jackie *does not reply. She fetches the stepladder and puts it by the shelves.*

Jackie How's work?

Margaret Fine. How's yours?

Jackie Oh – okay. (*Pause.*) I'll climb, and pass you things.

They work.

Margaret I read an article at the hairdressers, about a girl who does silk-screen printing, in Sheffield. Rather like you.

Jackie I don't do silk-screen printing. (*Pause. Passes a frame.*) – What a serious child you were!

Margaret (*looks at it*) On the beach at Scarborough. I was six years old. I remember Father wanted a nice one . . .

Jackie 'The highest standard', he'd always say to me.

Margaret 1937. I remember Father kissing me that day, and saying, 'You're nearly grown up now.' He didn't kiss me after that. (*Pause.*) If you left a bit of butter on your plate, it was either Mother on at you.about rationing, or Father would tell us again, how he started his business with a tin of boot polish, cleaning gentlemen's shoes on the steps of the Royal Exchange. What that had to do with butter, I really don't know.

Jackie (*lifts down a silver rose bowl*) The rose bowl. 'Manchester Business Award, 1949'.

Margaret He took me to the Exchange once, to look at his shares. Young women had to wait outside, of course. (*She has a spasm of pain.*)

Jackie Mummy – is it upsetting you? – Sit down for a bit.

Margaret (*fighting pain*) So much to do. (*Continues packing.*)

Jackie *looks worried.*

Next shelf, Jackie.

Jackie The pottery duck I made – look.

Margaret Rosie made that.

Jackie No, I made it for Grandad.

Margaret I think I should know.

Jackie Mummy I –

Margaret *has another spasm of pain.*

Please stop doing things for a moment.

Margaret It's just menopause. Cramps . . . (*She sits.*)

Jackie It shouldn't do that to you. Have you seen a doctor?

Margaret Surgery hours are nine till six. I'm working then.

Pause.

Jackie Rosie's very energetic . . .

Margaret She's like you.

Jackie . . . I meant it Mummy, about school holidays.

Margaret And how would you cope, the hours you work?

Jackie (*pause*) I could time share with Sandra at the City Art Gallery. I asked her. – She's got two small children now.

Pause.

Margaret All Rosie's schoolfriends are in London.

Pause.

Jackie It was just an offer. (*Clumsily.*) If you ever feel you can't cope –

Margaret What are you suggesting?!

Jackie Mummy, I want to ask you – (*Stops.*)

Margaret (*pause*) What?

They look at each other. Long pause.

Jackie Let's get on.

Margaret *gets up,* **Jackie** *climbs stepladder.*

When I've sold this house and invested the money for everyone, you won't have to work so hard.

Margaret I have to work. There's always something. I don't have your attitude to the future, Jackie.

Jackie (*pause.* **Jackie** *at top shelf*) That's everything. – No, what's this? (*Lifts down an old chocolate box. Opens it.*) – Look, a Victorian photograph! The frame's made of shells . . .

Margaret (*pauses*) That's mother's mother.

Jackie (*excited*) Is it? Look at that stiff black dress – and the high collar.

Margaret Goitre. Women over thirty never showed their necks in those days. Swellings. Hormone problem. No proper medicine to control it.

Jackie Why hasn't Granny ever showed us this?

Margaret (*pause*) Jack didn't like it. (*Pause.*) Mother grew up in what she calls – reduced circumstances . . . Her mother wasn't married.

Jackie – *stunned.*

I found out in a letter once.

Jackie (*fury*) How could you?

Margaret What?

Jackie Never tell me!

Margaret It wouldn't have made any difference, Jackie.

Jackie You know it would! (*Angry tears.*) Mummy –

A moment. **Jackie** *can't speak. Suddenly* **Rosie** *bursts into the room with a sheet over her head.*

Rosie Whoo-oo-oo! I'm a ghost.

Jackie Oh – (*She drops the framed photo, which breaks.*) Look what you made me do!

Rosie Sorry.

Margaret What on earth are you doing Rosie? – Where's Mother?

Rosie We're folding sheets. The landing's a snow storm.

Margaret (*weary*) Oh dear. I'd better go and look. – Jackie, you pick up the pieces. (*She exits.*)

Rosie Never mind Jackie. (*Kisses her.*) Look. Gran's cut holes for eyes in this sheet. She's done one for herself too, that'll give Mum a fright.

Jackie (*laughs*) Oh Rosie . . .

Rosie What?

Jackie I don't know . . .

Rosie What's up?

Jackie *fights tears. After a moment.*

Jackie Rosie, you must understand – (*Slight pause.*) Mummy has – a lot to cope with.

Rosie Oh, she's been telling you about Dad, hasn't she.

Jackie What about Dad?

Rosie Don't sound so worried. Why d'you always think things are your fault, Jackie?

Jackie – Does Mum work late?

Rosie Yeah. She's doing some new computer course in the evenings.

Jackie Does Dad mind?

Rosie Yeah, Mum drives him spare. They have rows a lot.

Jackie (*anxious*) What about?

Rosie Oh I dunno, the washing or something. I just put my Walkman on.

Jackie Poor Mummy . . . why didn't she tell me about it?

Rosie Well she doesn't want you to know she's messed things up. – C'mon, help me rip this sheet.

Jackie What for?

They rip the sheet in half.

Rosie A banner. We're doing a Greenham protest outside the physics lab at school.

Jackie Why?

Rosie Secrecy kills. (*Pause.*) – Nuclear secrecy. (*Holds out half sheet.*) – Here, you can make one too.

Jackie (*holds up sheet*) 'Sorry Mummy'.

Rosie (*pause*) How old are you?

Jackie Thirty. Why?

Rosie You should stop that sort of thing now, or you never will. You should hear Mum's 'I'm sorry' voice on the phone to Gran.

Jackie Don't you worry about what Mummy thinks?

Rosie I worry about nuclear war, and not getting a job, and whether Mr Walsh the physics teacher fancies me. Mum doesn't understand.

Jackie Fancy not worrying.

Rosie He's old enough to be my Dad. Mega creepy. – You're old enough to be my Mum! (*Pause.*) I'm glad you're not.

Jackie Why?

Rosie Because it would be a mega-pain having to live up to you. Grandad used to go on and on about you, you know.

Jackie He disapproved of me.

Rosie He didn't.

Jackie I'm not how he thinks a woman should be.

Rosie That's what he liked! You are dumb.

Jackie (*amazed*) It wasn't admiration you know, his will! It was revenge.

Rosie How?

Jackie I'd escaped. Families. – Nearly. He's made me responsible for all of you now.

Rosie (*pause*) You are thick. He left you the money so you can open a gallery of your own.

Jackie (*as she takes this in*) What would you do with the money Grandad left?

Rosie I'd buy a baseball jacket instead of this yucky anorak Mum makes me wear. I wouldn't give it all to Mum and Gran, like you. I'd give some to Greenpeace. – C'mon, let's go in the garden and practise our banners.

Rosie *opens the French windows and runs out swirling the sheet like a flag.* **Jackie** *hesitates.* **Doris** *enters, carrying a half-filled binliner.*

Doris There's some washing flapping in the garden.

Jackie It's Rosie. She wants to change the world. (*Pulls French windows shut.*)

Doris You used to be like that.

Jackie Have I changed so much?

Doris (*watches* **Rosie**) It was thick snow, that winter you came to stay. After Margaret had taken Rosie. – Not that you were in much of a state to enjoy Christmas.

Jackie You've still got my letter?

Doris Of course.

Jackie – Rosie must have it the day she's sixteen.

Doris Oh you make me so angry, Jackie! – You have to ask for what you want.

Jackie Granny, I can't!

Doris You can.

Jackie But Mummy's got so much to – it's not a good time for her.

Doris There's always an excuse. (*Pause.*) I never did ask for what I wanted. Resentment is a terrible thing, Jackie. You don't want to be resenting somebody at the end of your life.

Jackie (*avoiding this*) What's in the binliner?

Doris (*stiffly*) The pale blue curtains from the bedroom.

Jackie Oh good. Pale blue's your favourite, isn't it.

Doris Jack chose all the colours in this house (*Slight pause.*) Very artistic, visitors used to say. (*Pause.*) Scarlet, I'll have in my new house (*Pause.*)

Enter **Margaret** *carrying a binliner. As she puts it down.*

Margaret Everything in the binliner is for Oxfam.

Doris Nothing ventured, Jackie.

Jackie Mummy . . .

Margaret Jackie, if you're not doing anything, there's the spare room to sort out.

Jackie Yes, Mummy.

There is a rumbling noise beyond the hall.

Doris I told you that boiler wasn't right, Margaret.

Margaret Yes Mother. (*She exits.*)

Jackie (*picks up binliner with curtains which* **Doris** *brought in*) Shall I put these curtains with the stuff for Oxfam, Granny?

Doris There's something else in that bag, Jackie. Some things you left with me once.

Jackie What?

Doris The baby clothes.

Jackie (*pause – can't cope*) I'd better go and see if everything's all right in the kitchen.

Doris Are you going to give them away?

Jackie No. – Thank you, for keeping them safe, Granny.

Jackie *exits.* **Doris** *opens the French windows.*

Doris Rosie!

Rosie *comes in laughing and breathless, with the banner.*

Doris It's a waste of time. The world's going to end soon, I saw it on the television.

Rosie That's only the official view, you mustn't believe them . . . But it was scary when it blew up, wasn't it?

Margaret (*entering*) What's blown up, Rosie dear?

Rosie The world.

Margaret Oh. That's all right. I thought it was something else.

Doris What?

Margaret Nothing, Mother.

Doris We thought perhaps the kitchen ceiling had come down. Jackie went to have a look. She's so good at that sort of thing.

Margaret (*wearily*) Yes Mother. (*Exits.*)

Doris They work too hard.

Rosie You shouldn't wind them up.

Doris You should be helping them.

Rosie They'd only say I was more trouble.

They smile.

Doris I'll show you something. (*Pulls the dustsheet of the piano from Act One.*)

Rosie (*pause*) It's the piano.

Doris Don't you like it?

Rosie We've got a synth at school.

Doris I had a friend called Cynth.

Rosie What's this? (*Picks up a plate on top of the piano.*)

Doris It's a salver. Jack's employees gave it him on his retirement. It's only plate, of course.

Rosie (*sniffs*) The silver smells funny. I hate old things.

Doris You hate dead things, not old things, Rosie. (*Pause.*) So do I. (*Pause.*) I'm old.

Rosie Hold this. So you can see your face in it. (**Doris** *holds the plate.*) Sit down on the piano stool. (**Doris** *does so.*)

Doris What are you going to do?

Rosie Aha. Close your eyes.

Rosie *stands behind her and puts her hands on* **Doris's** *cheeks, gently pulling the skin back and taut.*

Rosie Smooth the wrinkles away . . .

Doris Nice warm hands, Rosie.

Rosie Now open your eyes, Gran.

Doris Oh! (*She studies her reflection.*)

Rosie There, see. You're not old really. Only on the surface. (*A moment. Then* **Rosie** *lets go.*) My outside's the same as my inside. That's why when I talk Mum thinks I'm being rude.

Doris (*gets up, puts the salver in the box*) When you're old . . . if you're rude . . . they just think your mind is going. (*Pause.*) They never understand that it's anger. (*Pause.*) Help me polish the piano.

Rosie Do I have to?

Doris There's some dusters and polish in Margaret's holdall.

Rosie (*passes them. Reads tin*) 'Bradley's beeswax.' With a picture of a bee. Here.

Doris That's Jack's firm, of course. (*Tries, then.*) Can you unscrew it?

Rosie (*does so*) What was your surname, Gran?

Doris Partington. Here, you take this cloth, and do the legs.

Rosie *does.*

They polish the piano during the following.

Rosie We're doing a project about you at school.

Doris About me?

Rosie Yeah, you're working class Lancashire, aren't you?

Doris Do I look like it?

Rosie Yeah . . . (*As if from school book.*) 'Oldham families were all cotton or paper. Despite the decline in the manufacturing industries, community spirit remained strong.'

Doris (*reminiscing*) You'd give a neighbour a bit of sugar, bit of soap, what they needed. When the King came, we scooped up the manure for the tomatoes. Pride costs nothing.

Rosie That's what they said on the documentary we saw at school.

Doris Did they now. You've missed a bit there, see. When Mother and I arrived in Jubilee Street, the landlady, a big woman, arms like beef, though she wore fancy hats, said 'I didn't know you had a babby'. 'You never asked', said Mother. She did! And that was that.

Rosie You didn't have a Dad?

Doris No.

Rosie Does Mum know?

Doris No.

Rosie Can it be our secret?

Doris If you like, Rosie. Of course people gossiped, but the girl next door was illegitimate too, it was more common than they put on those documentaries. I was instilled. To get on. Work hard and you will rise like bread, my mother said – Are you polishing that, or just resting your arm? – No one's ever told me what to do. Of course by the time I met Jack the neighbourhood wasn't what it used to be. Wicked things, even in Oldham. Well, there was the Depression. When you've got no job you lose a sense of things. But we worked. We moved up. To Cheadle Hulme! (*Pause.*) It was very – (*Pause.*) – snob. When Jack's parents came visiting I used to borrow the silver teapot from Next Door. Got in a fix one day, because Next Door's in-laws popped by the same afternoon. We had to pass it through the window, back and forth. (*Pause.*) I never used bicarb, for my scones, just elbow. (*Rubs.*) There now. We can see our faces in it. (*Pause. Both admire it.*) It will fetch quite a bit, I fancy.

Rosie You can sell pianos through the small-ads.

Doris Jackie's organised an auction, hasn't she? Put these cloths away, they're soiled now.

Rosie *opens* **Margaret***'s binliner, thinking it's rubbish.*

Doris That's not rubbish –

Rosie Hey it's full of clothes! (*Tips the binliner all over the floor. Picks some up.*) Cheesecloth and flares! Yuck. I didn't know you were a hippy once, Gran.

Doris Oh quite a – what's the word – 'swinger'.

Rosie No kidding?

Doris No. (*Pause.*) Those were Jackie's – she came to stay with us once, left some things she didn't need any more.

Rosie Aren't they revolting! My big sister in these! (*Pulls out the ski pants* **Margaret** *wore in Act One, Scene Seven.*) Oh, can I have these ski pants?

Doris You can have what you like. Margaret obviously doesn't care for any of them. Everything's throwaway now, of course.

Rosie But these are brill Gran! mega trendy!

Rosie *pulls ski pants over her tights and skirt.*

Doris You don't want those slacks. There's a nice beige skirt here, see love. (*Picks out skirt she wore in Act One, Scene Seven.*) Margaret bought those . . . 'Pants' . . . (*Disdain.*) They're American.

Rosie Are they real fifties?

Doris There's generations here, all mixed up, if you poke about. (*Rummages in binliner.*)

Margaret *re-enters and goes to her holdall.*

Margaret Don't say I didn't bring rubber gloves . . .

She pulls a pair from her holdall and puts them on during:

Rosie Mum, look! (*Silence.*) – D'you recognise them? (*Silence.*) Gee, ah simply must do mah nails! (**Rosie** *parades about.*) – Mum?

Margaret Rosie we haven't time for dressing up games.

Doris I think they rather suit her, Margaret.

Rosie They're really sexy. I can't imagine you fitting into these, Mum! – Did she look nice in them, Gran?

Pause.

Margaret Did I Mother?

Pause.

Rosie Can't you remember that far back?

Doris You only remember what you want.

Margaret Rosie, clear up this mess. We're going as soon as Jackie's fixed the boiler. (*She exits.*)

Rosie I'm keeping these on for going home. Will you help me put my hair up, like they did?

Doris (*helps* **Rosie** *put her hair up*) A beehive? Sugar and water you need for that.

Rosie (*delight*) – Like a punk!

They are stuffing clothes back into the binliner.

(*Amused.*) – Shall I keep this hippy stuff to show Jackie?

Doris I wouldn't bother.

Rosie Why not? – Really embarrass her!

Doris Not all memories are pleasant. (*Beat.*)

Rosie We should hide some clothes in the cellar, for someone to find in a hundred years . . .

Doris ties the binliner shut. **Rosie** *reaches for the other one.*

Rosie What's in here?

Doris – Oh, just some old curtains.

Rosie (*opens it*) What sweet little baby clothes! (*Tips them all over the floor.*) – You're not looking, Gran!

Doris Put those back in the bag, Rosie.

Rosie I want this one with the little rabbits on.

Doris No. That belongs to Jackie.

Rosie I'll ask Jackie then.

Doris I should have known . . .

Enter **Jackie,** *distracted.*

Jackie Did I leave the stepladder in here?

She stops, seeing the baby clothes everywhere.

Rosie (*holds up rabbit dress*) Look what I found!

Jackie (*pause*) Not your rabbit dress.

Rosie – Mine? Gran, you said this was Jackie's.

Doris Did I? Well, you ask Jackie.

Rosie *looks at* **Jackie.**

Jackie (*slowly*) I bought it for you, Rosie.

Margaret (*calls from the hall*) Jackie!

Rosie *whips the rabbit dress behind her just as* **Margaret** *enters on the line.*

Margaret Are you helping me or not?

She stops and takes in the scene.

Rosie Guess what Mum, you'll never guess!

Margaret (*terror*) What.

Rosie GUESS!

(*She brings out the rabbit dress from behind her back.*) – My baby dress! (*Pause.*) And guess what Jackie told me –

Margaret (*giddy*) No . . .

Jackie It's okay everyone. Mummy it's okay.

She goes to **Margaret** *but they can't hold each other.*

Rosie What?

Jackie Mummy's . . . not feeling well. Are you?

Margaret I'm perfectly all right!

Stasis.

Doris I think I've had enough for today.

Jackie Yes, it's getting late, isn't it.

Rosie It's half past five, you wallies!

Margaret Rosie, don't shout.

Jackie Mummy, are you all right?

Doris I expect she's been overdoing it.

Margaret Rosie put those baby clothes in the bag for Oxfam.

Rosie Oh Mum, don't be BORING.

Jackie Rosie! She's just sitting down.

Rosie I CAN SEE SHE'S SITTING DOWN!

Doris You're tired, dear.

Rosie I'm NOT TIRED!

Jackie You are!

Rosie Not you too!

Doris Margaret, have you seen my piano?

Margaret It's over there, Mother.

Doris I KNOW. I'm talking about the polish. You've not even noticed have you?

Margaret Oh MOTHER! What did you do that for? It'll only need poishing again after the move.

Doris I'm selling it. At the auction.

Margaret But it's the only thing Father left for you.

Doris It was mine anyway. I bought it with my savings from teaching, when I got married. (*Pause.*) You never knew, did you?

Margaret You can't . . .

Rosie 'Course she can.

Jackie Food; everyone into the car.

Rosie I'm not hungry yet.

Margaret Mother needs to have her tea promptly, don't you dear?

Doris Oh I'm no trouble. I shall have a boiled egg.

Rosie Can we go to McDonald's? Yeah!

Jackie We're all going to my flat.

Margaret You don't cook, Jackie.

Jackie We're getting a take-out Indian. There's a good place on the Stockport Road.

Margaret Mother can't possibly chew spare ribs.

Doris Chew what?

Rosie I hate curry. I want a McDonald's. Can I keep these on?

Doris Yes.

Margaret No. Have you got your handbag, Mother?

Doris I don't need helping, thank you. Are you going home in rubber gloves?

Jackie Mummy, are you okay to drive, if I take the van?

Margaret (*picks up thermos and thermos cup*) Does anyone want this tea . . . ?

Rosie Mu-um, it's cold. – Knowing you, you'll probably take it home and save it for tomorrow.

Margaret Rosie! (*She tips tea into the thermos and screws cup on.*)

Jackie I'll take these out to the van. (*Goes to the binliners. Sees a dress lying behind them.*) What's this dress? I didn't see it before – it looks like an original 1920s!

Doris I think there was a tea stain . . . no, it was a grass stain . . . I wore that frock the day that Jack proposed.

Jackie Do you want to keep it?

Jackie *hesitates, holding up the dress. No response. She puts it in the binliner and ties it shut.*

Margaret I'm going to check the windows and turn the power off. You two get in the car. (*Exits.*)

Jackie I'll see you both back at my flat. (*Hesitates.*) Look at you with your hair up like that, Rosie! I wish you were still a baby. You were so sweet . . .

Rosie Was I?

Doris There was a time for babies, Jackie, and it's gone.

Rosie Ow, Jackie you always hug too hard!

Doris Truth will out, Jackie. Don't say I didn't warn you.

Rosie C'mon Gran, let's go.

Jackie *looks at* Doris, *picks up binliners and goes.*

Doris Come along Rosie, put your anorak on.

As Doris *helps* Rosie *into her anorak, the room is suddenly plunged into darkness.*

Doris Oh!

Rosie I left the big torch on the landing! – Wait there, Gran. (*Exits.*)

Doris (*goes to French windows. Sound of wind*) Jack? Jack . . . You should see how the roses have all blown down in the garden . . . crushed . . . You rattle like a dry pod, now. Skin on your skull like frayed paper. (*Pause.*) I tried so hard, even in those last few years . . . Something nourishing and not difficult to chew . . . The tray pushed aside on your bed. You did that deliberately, didn't you? (*Pause.*) When you died and the nurses left me alone with you, to pray I suppose, I climbed into bed beside you, yes I did, lay beside you then . . . the sun was shining through the window, hot; only you were cold as ice.

Rosie (*re-enters, carrying a round wooden board; also the flashlight, which she swings around the room until the beam comes to rest on* **Doris**'s *face.* **Doris** *has been crying.*) – Gran? . . .

Doris Give me a minute. I'll put my hat and gloves on.

Rosie Gran? Hurry, what are you doing?

Car horn honks outside.

Doris Are they waiting for us?

Rosie (*gently*) You haven't got any gloves . . . oh Gran. (*Goes to* **Doris**. *A split second of hesitation.*)

Doris Don't kiss –

Rosie Yes! (**Rosie** *kisses* **Doris**. **Doris** *strokes* **Rosie**'s *hair.*)

Doris Lovely hair . . . mine are all old grey hairs . . .

Rosie (*holds up a wooden board*) Look, Gran, look what I found in the spare room. What is it?

Doris Solitaire. Why, that was my mother's, she gave it me. It's a game. I used to sit and play it in the evenings, while Jack read the papers. You have to get rid of all the marbles from the holes in the board, until there is just one left, in the centre. Solitaire.

Car horn sounds again.

Rosie Can we take it with us?

Doris Yes, if you want, Rosie.

Rosie Will you show me how to do it?

Doris If you come and visit me. Put your hood up now, it's snowing out.

Rosie *takes the Solitaire board and flashlight. She swings the beam round the room one last time. As they move to go, the sound of wind and snow increases.*

Blackout.

Interval.

Act Three

Scene One

The backyard of Doris's terrace house in Oldham, early April 1987. Doris is 87, wears a floral overall; Margaret is 56, dressed in the sensible suit she wears to work, wearing an apron she has borrowed from Doris. They are chatting as they come out of the back kitchen door, Doris guiding Margaret. Margaret is carrying a tray of small geraniums in pots, Doris carrying a kneeler. They kneel beside a tub and a bag of potting compost.

Doris See dear, all those are from the one plant I brought with me from Cheadle Hulme.

Margaret I've had mine in the kitchen all winter, but they've not done so well.

Doris Oh you have to cut them right down until they're just dry sticks, then all of a sudden, it seems, they start producing new leaves.

Margaret They'll look lovely here.

Doris I've had a postcard from Rosie. She and Jackie seem to be having a lovely time.

Margaret Yes. It's very quiet at home.

Pause. **Margaret** *continues planting a geranium in the tub.*

Doris You look thinner. Are you eating properly?

Margaret What do you mean?

Doris Don't crowd the roots – Well – you coming all the way from London like this – on a Tuesday!

Margaret Can't I even come and see you for the day without –

Doris Usually you're so busy, at that office . . . never have time to come and visit.

Margaret Yes well I took the day off!

Doris No need to snap dear.

Pause. **Margaret** *digs a hole.*

Margaret You've transformed this backyard, I must say. The trellis is nice.

Doris Yes, I'm quite proud, it's only five years since the move. Cheadle Hulme will be a mass of blossom, now, of course. The jasmine hasn't done very well, but then it's been such a Spring.

Margaret Good. (*Pause.*) I mean, sorry, yes. – It's been awful, Spring, hasn't it.

Doris How are your geranium tubs doing?

Margaret Mmm.

Doris I ate my shoe this afternoon.

Margaret Yes. (*Picks a leaf, stares at it.*)

Doris Margaret, you're not listening to a word I'm saying, are you?

Margaret Of course . . .

Doris What's wrong, Margaret?

Margaret What do you mean, what's wrong?

Doris You're upset.

Margaret I'm probably upset because you're accusing me of being upset.

Doris (*smoothly*) I'm not accusing you. Don't take umbrage.

Margaret Really Mother. I make the effort to come here for a friendly visit and you react as though there's something wrong! Can't I even have a normal conversation with my own Mother?

Doris I don't know, dear.

Margaret What do you mean, you don't know? (*Pause.*) And don't call me 'dear'!

Doris Trains from London are so expensive at this time of day.

Margaret There, see? We can't even talk without the housekeeping coming into it.

Doris (*pause. Gently*) What is it dear? It's Ken, isn't it (*Silence.*)
. . . He's not been made redundant? (*Silence.*)

Margaret (*pause*) I don't know.

Doris What do you mean, you don't know.

Margaret I haven't seen Ken for a week, Mother. (*Pause.*) I don't
think it's another woman. He's not like that. And we've always
been very happy. I know it happens to one in three marriages these
days, but – you don't think of yourself as a statistic, do you?
(*Pause.*) Mummy, I still want him.

Doris Your Father . . . stopped 'wanting me', many years ago. One
didn't divorce, then. I thought if I persisted in loving him . . . I
wanted to – to be desired. (*Pause.*) The night before he died, we
embraced. He held my hand; he said that he loved me most that
night. I believed him . . . Was it worth it, I ask myself? (*Silence.*)
You've made more of your life. A job and that.

Margaret Exactly. It's all my fault. He loved me, Mother . . . but
he didn't want to share me.

Doris With who?

Margaret With the job. Trying to work and look after Rosie . . .
Well I had to work, London's so expensive now. (*Pause.*) But Ken
married a wife, not a working mother.

Doris You expected too much. So did I. And Jackie expects even
more. (*Pause.*) My father turned up once, after we'd moved to
Jubilee Street. Mother took him back, of course. I saw the marks,
when she was bathing in front of the fire. She said it was because
he loved her so much, he hugged her too tight. (*Pause.*) When I
think about Jack, I think, well, I was lucky really.

Doris *gently lowers the geranium plant into the hole* **Margaret** *has
dug.* **Margaret** *pats soil around it.*

Doris Come in the cottage with me, dear. There's something I want
to give you. (*Pause.*) You've never seen a photograph of my
Mother, have you?

Margaret (*a white lie*) No.

Margaret *stands and helps* **Doris** *stand.* **Doris** *takes* **Margaret** *by the arm as they go in.*

Scene Two

Croydon, London, early April 1987, four days later. A bright sunny morning in **Margaret's** *office, but traffic noise outside. A desk, a telephone, a typewriter, a pot of geraniums and a photo frame.* **Margaret** *is 56,* **Jackie** *is 34,* **Rosie** *is 15½.*

Margaret *is seated, uncovering the typewriter. She wears a sensible suit as in the previous scene.*

Rosie (*enters with an orange kite and a bundle of letters, which she puts on* **Margaret's** *desk. She wears colourful and sophisticated holiday clothes*) Morning post, Mrs Metcalfe.

Margaret Rosie! What on earth are you doing here?

Rosie (*kisses* **Margaret.** *Makes the kite swoop round the office space*) Look! Isn't it beautiful!

Margaret Have you been home yet?

Rosie No. We came straight from Gatwick, all the way in a taxi, can you imagine! But Jackie says when it's important you have to do these things.

Margaret (*touching her hair*) Is she here too?

Rosie Yes. Only she's gone in the third floor Ladies to change into her Art Dealer dress. She doesn't want you to see her looking a mess.

Margaret Is she going straight back to work?

Rosie There's some meeting about the future of her gallery, with the Manchester City Council. (*She swoops the kite.*)

Margaret But you've both been travelling all night!

Rosie So?

Margaret You'd better get that out of sight before Mr Reece arrives at nine.

Rosie Don't you like it? Such style, the Italians.

Margaret How was Venice?

Rosie Brilliant! 'Fettucine alla casa, va bene?'! The food was marvellous. Dad would have hated it!

Margaret I'm sure.

Rosie I can't believe it's only two weeks! What have you been up to? You didn't clean my room?

Margaret I went to visit Granny.

Rosie I sent her a postcard of the beach where we flew this kite. Also we brought some Chianti back for Dad, and you'll never guess what we've brought you! Did Dad water my tomatoes?

Margaret (*pause*) Dad's gone away for the week. What did you like best in Venice?

Rosie Oh, definitely the carnival. We stayed up all night, everyone wore masks like birds, that's when I saw the kites. We had breakfast at San Marco's, and this man fell in love with Jackie, so I just stared into the canal and ordered another cappucino, and pretended I was waiting for a gondola. And then it turned out it was me he fancied, and Jackie got very cross with him in Italian, and we had to leave.

Margaret I hope you didn't stay up every night?

Rosie Oh yes – Mum, of course not. I mean – Jackie's so sweet, she was trying so hard to be like you.

Margaret Like me?

Rosie Yes. I can't think of anyone less like a mother! (*Pause.*) You know Mum, sometimes you have to be a bit silly with Jackie just to get her to relax. She needs . . .

Margaret What does she need?

Rosie . . . I don't know . . . it's hard to explain. (*Thinks.*) She's so restless: she's always looking for something to do. We spent a whole day trekking round museums but she could never find the picture she wanted. After I'd got this kite, we went to this incredible long beach, ran for miles. (*Swoops kite.*) We were shouting because of the wind, and Jackie got the kite to do a perfect circle in the sky . . . Oh Mum, it was such a brilliant day . . . Will you stop opening letters for a minute –

Margaret I'm at work.

Rosie Yes, but I have to tell you something! Oh Mum, it's incredible!

Margaret What dear?

Rosie Well, I asked Jackie – I could't believe she'd agree – I want to go and live with her in Manchester!

Margaret (*long pause*) What about your exams?

Rosie Oh, I won't go till the summer, of course. Anyway, Jackie says we have to discuss it with you and Dad first. (*Pause.*) Mum . . . ?

Margaret You've no idea. Jackie can't cook, she'll forget to wash your clothes . . .

Rosie I know! She's so useless at most things. Not like you. (*Pause.*) She needs me. (*Pause.*) I'll come back and visit, lots.

Margaret Whenever you can afford the fare.

Rosie Oh Jackie will pay. She says we'll both visit. She comes to London all the time, anyway.

Margaret Does she?

Rosie (*cuts in*) You said! Don't you remember? You promised, after my exams I could do whatever I wanted.

Margaret (*long pause*) Yes, I did. (*Turns away, afraid she's going to cry.*) I've got to . . . write a letter, Rosie, can you wait outside a minute . . .

Rosie exits, swooping the kite as she goes. Jackie and Rosie meet in the corridor. Jackie is wearing a print dress, carrying a Chinese lacquered briefcase and a blue kite.

Rosie Don't go in. (*Surveys* **Jackie**.) You've spoiled it now, Miss Executive. You should go to work wearing that turquoise thing.

Jackie That was a beach dress.

Rosie Suited you much better.

Jackie It's an incredibly important meeting.

Rosie All the more reason to let them see what you're really like.

Jackie I can't start now.

Rosie You could. If you really wanted. Come outside and fly this kite with me.

Jackie I want to see Mummy.

Rosie She's busy.

Jackie I'll sit in her office and prepare for my meeting.

Rosie See – now you're being all business woman again!

Jackie Calm down. You're not at home now.

Rosie Mum isn't like you when she's at work. (*Goes, swooping the kite.*)

Jackie (*enters the office*) Mummy! I'm sorry. Didn't you get the message? The delay was twelve hours in the end, airport like an oven.

Margaret Rosie's hopelessly over-excited.

Jackie I know Mummy, I couldn't get her to sleep. But she's been so good all holiday, you don't need to worry. She's very sensible for fifteen. Wouldn't let me swim too far out.

Margaret She'll be tired for the first day of term now.

Jackie That's three days away!

Margaret There's all her clothes to wash.

Jackie I'd do it, but I've . . .

Margaret Got to go back to Manchester for a meeting.

Jackie (*pause*) Rosie can wash her own things. She did all our clothes one evening, fixed up a line on the balcony.

Margaret It's an adventure with you. (*Pause.*) You should see her bedroom, it's like a junkyard – clothes, glue, paint.

Jackie She's very creative. Kept writing poetry in the restaurant.

Margaret She's full of crazy ideas. (*Testing* **Jackie**.)

Jackie (*pause. Cautious*) Is she? (*No reply from* **Margaret**.) It's just her energy, isn't it.

Margaret Well of course with you . . .

Jackie She talks about you a lot.

Margaret What about?

Jackie Oh, I only mean your job. She wanted to show me all round where you work.

Margaret Did she?

Jackie You didn't tell me you were promoted last year. (*Looks over* **Margaret**'s *shoulder at the letters she is opening.*)

Margaret It's nothing glamorous.

Jackie You know I'd be useless at this. My typing's awful . . . Do you have to reply to all these?

Margaret Mr Reece dictates, I spend the rest of the morning unravelling his grammar, otherwise British Microwaves would never have any export trade. These young graduates.

Jackie I hope they pay you the right scale. You're the one who does all the work.

Margaret I'm only his personal assistant.

Jackie Don't say 'only'.

Margaret Oh I was lucky. My typing speeds are very ordinary. It's only that I've got Pitman's Classic and most of the girls don't learn shorthand these days.

Jackie I'm sure it's other qualities got you this job, Mummy.

Margaret (*pause. Pleased*) It's funny, hearing 'Mummy' in this place. You do a job, people treat you differently.

Jackie It's only how you treat yourself.

Margaret (*pause*) You look radiant dear.

Jackie Swimming and sea air. (*Quiet.*) Bit of sun, Mummy. Do you good, too.

Margaret (*quiet*) Sat in the garden this weekend. Been very . . . Been a relief, you having Rosie for these two weeks.

Jackie (*pause*) I hope you kept the appointment? She's a nice woman, isn't she?

Margaret It was a very expensive looking waiting room.

Jackie Mummy, I asked you to see the specialist, not the wallpaper. What did she say?

Margaret Oh – Nothing much.

Jackie Did she do some tests?

Margaret No.

Jackie No?

Margaret Says I'm fine. Just menopause, probably.

Jackie (*pause*) Honestly?

Margaret (*pause*) What do you mean?

Jackie Well – (*Pause.*) – That's such a relief! (*Laughs.*) Oh Mummy. We even got a taxi all the way here!

Margaret (*pause*) Now you can go and catch your train to Manchester, can't you.

Jackie Mum . . . May Bank holiday, come and stay with me. Just you, and we'll . . .

Margaret Fly kites.

Jackie (*gives her the blue kite*) Oh yes, Rosie and I bought you a kite. She says Daddy will show you how to fly it, but I said you're an expert. Do you remember, how you took me flying kites in

Richmond Park, and once it got stuck in a chestnut tree, and all the conkers came down?

Margaret I thought you'd wiped out that little girl.

Jackie So did I. Rosie won't. She'll have kites in her office, or whatever. (*Pause.*) I used to wear suits, when I first started my job. (*Bends and picks up a photo frame*) Is this Cornwall? . . . Oh can I have a copy? Doesn't Rosie look sweet!

Margaret (*pause*) Rosie's told me, Jackie.

Jackie (*terrified*) I wasn't going to –

Margaret No, I except you had another date planned when you were going to tell me that you'd like Rosie back. Or perhaps you were just going to tell me over the phone.

Jackie . . . You need time, to decide . . . in the summer –

Margaret It's not my decision. It's Rosie's. And she's made her mind up. (*Pause.*) I knew she'd say it one day. Like one of those fairytales.

Jackie You haven't told her!

Margaret Of course not. She still thinks you're big sister, that's why it's so magical to her.

Jackie We were running along this dazzling beach. I thought, is that what I've missed?

Margaret Years and years and years you've lost, Jackie. Birthdays and first snowman and learning to ride a bicycle and new front teeth. You can't pull them back.

Jackie I can make up for it – somehow –

Margaret You can't. Those are my years.

Jackie She must remember – I visited!

Margaret Treats, she's had with you. A day here and there. That never fooled her. But I let it fool you. I'm the woman who sat up all night with the sick child, who didn't mind all her best crockery getting broken over the years.

Jackie Mummy . . .

Margaret (*long pause. Cool*) What time's your train?

Jackie 9.45 – no – I could get the 10.45.

Margaret You mustn't miss your meeting.

Jackie It would give us another hour. I wish we weren't in your office! (*Panics.*) Where's Rosie gone?

Margaret Are you going to catch that train, or stay here? You can't do both.

Pause. **Jackie** *agonises.*

Margaret I'll phone you a taxi. (**Margaret** *dials, waits, the line is engaged.*)

Jackie (*quietly*) You know Mummy, the Gallery and everything, I couldn't have done it without you. You can't be a mother and then cancel Christmas to be in New York.

Margaret (*telephone connects*) Taxi to East Croydon station please, immediately. British Microwaves, front entrance. (*Puts receiver down.*)

Jackie Come and stay, show me how you do things, how Rosie would like her room decorated.

Margaret No Jackie, I shall just put a label around Rosie's neck, and send her Red Star. (*Doesn't look at* **Jackie** *any more, busies herself with papers.*) It's gone nine. I wonder where Mr Reece is?

Jackie *runs out of the room.*

Margaret (*bursts into tears. Telephone rings*) Hello? Hello. Yes, I'll be with you directly. (*Puts down the receiver.*) Oh God, my mascara – all over the letters. (*Picks up notebook to go.*) It will be strange. I'm a single woman again. (*Calms herself.*) I'll oversleep. (*Hesitates then dials telephone.*) Hello? Manchester City Art Gallery? Yes, I'd like to leave a message for Jackie Metcalfe. Just say – (*Pause.*) – May Bank Holiday will be fine. (*Puts phone down and walks out of the office. Blackout.*)

Scene Three

The Wasteland. Cats wail. Almost dark. We see the glint of faces and hands.

Jackie Harelip and eye of bat.

Rosie Poisoned dewdrop and tail of cat.

Jackie Put it in a monkey's hat.

Doris What's a monkey's hat?

Jackie Sssh!

Rosie You can't have harelip.

Jackie Sssh!

Doris Why?

Rosie It's something real. You get it. I've seen a lady with it in the opticians.

Doris What's it like?

Jackie Sssh! I can't con-centrate. This is a laboratory. (*Stirring twig potage.*)

Rosie It's a sort of slit in your mouth, goes up your nose.

Doris Eugh.

Rosie You're born with it. It means you're missing a bit in the head, too.

Jackie Shut up!

Doris Let's go and have a look!

Rosie Optician's closed.

Jackie (*mysteriously*) She didn't used to have it. It grew.

Rosie Honest?

Jackie Maybe *we* did it. (*Pause.*)

Rosie How could we . . .

Doris Could we?

Jackie (*grand*) I can tell you what her name is.

Rosie Go on.

Jackie Mrs Worsley.

Doris That's right!

Jackie See? Proves it. Our powers.

Doris What powers?

Jackie In the earth.

Rosie What happens to people when they die, then?

Jackie They rot. Worms go in their nose and out their eyeballs.

Doris No! (*Starts to cry.*) I don't want to do that–

Jackie It's too late.

Rosie I don't want to do that to Mum!

Jackie 'S too late. Was her idea.

Doris No!

Rosie No it wasn't, it was yours.

Doris Stop it!

Rosie Stop the spell.

Doris Make it go backwards!

Jackie You can't make someone's life go backwards.

Rosie I'm going to tell her – c'mon! (*Grabs* Doris *and they run off.*)

Doris Wasn't me!

Jackie She'll be dead when you get there.

Cats wail. The shadowy figure of Margaret *appears upstage.*

Jackie I didn't mean to do it! Don't leave me all alone!

She runs off.

Scene Four

Hospital, Twickenham, late May 1987. **Margaret** *in a hospital gown, with her hair scraped back. Her face is drawn, and very white. Under anaesthetic. She has become only a voice.*

Margaret I know the door is here somewhere, if only I could find it, the door to the garden . . . Here's a door . . . the bathroom! . . . What a cold wind blowing through here . . . Why, here we are, on its iron legs, the white enamel bath . . . cold on your bare flesh, even in summer . . . goosepimples . . . Father's made his fortune! But we still have to save hot water . . . Everything is a sacrifice in this house. Everything – is – sacrified for . . . Piano Tuition. Tu-ition . . . BUT! (*Whispers, conspiratorial.*) One must go to the bathroom and lock the door if one wants – needs – to CRY! . . . When you pull the plug out, the water gets sucked down with a roar . . . So they know I'm here . . . no privacy in this huge house . . . My parents are called, My parents are called . . . Sticks and Stones . . . When *I* have babies, they will be called Sugar and Spice and all things nice . . . I will give them everything they want, and they will love me (*Pause.*) . . . Mother? . . . Mummy . . . What happens when you die? . . . I wish they wouldn't keep opening the door, it's so cold . . . I'm sure I can find the garden, if I just keep going.

Lights fade on her. We hear a child crying, then a baby crying. Fade out.

Scene Five

The garden of **Ken** *and* **Margaret**'s *suburban semi in Raynes Park, London, late May 1987, early morning, 2 hours after Scene Four.* **Rosie** *sits on the swing beneath the cherry tree with the old red tranny wearing one of* **Ken**'s *jumpers, which is much too big, and jeans.* **Jackie** *runs across the garden, hot and grubby, carrying her lacquered briefcase, dressed for work. Both have been up all night.*

LBC Radio More congestion on the North Circular, meanwhile the overturned tanker is still blocking the Blackwall Tunnel. And it's coming up to 8 o'clock, a lovely May morning . . . Looking down the Euston Road, here's to the girl in that blue Mini, a thought from the Beatles . . . (*Plays 'All You Need Is Love'.*)

Jackie Rosie? . . .

Silence. Hold this for as long as possible while **Jackie** *has to cope with it.*

Rosie I hope you're a success, Jackie. A big, big success.

Jackie Rosie are you all right? Where's Daddy?

Rosie I hope lots of people came to your opening and thought your gallery was brill.

Jackie It was only twelve hours – I'd never have gone back to Manchester if I'd thought – after Daddy phoned last night, there were no more planes. I got the first plane I could this morning. If only . . .

Rosie In case you want to know, she died at 6.20 last night. Dad was with her. They said it was quicker at the end. It wasn't just stomach cancer, there were secondaries.

Jackie (*goes to hug* **Rosie** *who won't let her*) If only I'd been here with you . . .

Rosie (*turns away*) Did you sell lots of your paintings?

Jackie Rosie –

Rosie Did you?

Jackie I didn't sell any. I cancelled the opening.

Rosie I don't believe you. You'd never do that.

Silence.

Jackie What do we do . . . now? . . . I'll call a taxi to the hospital – do we have to take things – her birth certificate? . . . I don't know . . .

Rosie Dad's done all that. He's been brilliant, like it was before they split up. He knew where Mum kept the box that's got all the family stuff in it. Look – he said I could have this one – (*Holds out a photo.*) That's Mum holding me by the front door when I'd just arrived . . . And . . . (*Lays them on grass.*) – Here's Mum's birth certificate, . . . and here's mine.

Silence.

Jackie No.

Rosie So now I know.

Jackie (*desperate*) I was going to tell you – in five months – when you were sixteen . . . Mummy said to wait till after your exams, so as not to upset you . . .

Rosie (*has a handful of photos, throws them down one by one, except for one which she slips in her pocket*) 1972, my first birthday, 1973, my second birthday, Christmas 1975, 1976; then you were in South America, 1979 with the birthday cake, 1982 when we cleared Gran and Grandad's house, – and our holiday in Venice. (*Pause.*) Have them. Have them all.

Jackie Rosie – we've got to help each other now.

Rosie Why don't you go and get drunk, or whatever it is you lot do to show you're feeling something.

Jackie I wanted you to have opportunities I couldn't ever have given you.

Rosie No you didn't. You wanted your own life more than you wanted mine!

Jackie Don't!

Rosie If you were really my Mum you wouldn't have been able to give me away!

Jackie How dare you! (*Goes to hit* **Rosie** *but cannot.*) You're at the centre of everything I do! (*Slight pause.*) Mummy treated me as though I'd simply fallen over and cut my knee, – picked me up and said you'll be all right now, it won't show much. She wanted to make it all better. (*Quiet.*) . . . She was the one who wanted it kept secret . . . I WANTED you, Rosie. (*Angry.*) For the first time in my life I took care of myself – refused joints, did exercises, went to the clinic. (*Pause.*) 'It's a girl'. (*Smiles irresistibly.*) – After you'd gone I tried to lose that memory. (*Pause. Effort.*) Graham . . . your Father. (*Silence.*) He couldn't be there the day you were born, he had to be in Liverpool. He was married. (*Emphatic.*) He loved me, he loved you, you must believe that! (*Pause.*) He said he'd leave his wife, but I knew he wouldn't; there were two children, the youngest was only four . . . we'd agreed, separate lives, I wanted to bring you up. He sent money. (*Pause.*) I took you to Lyme Park one day, I saw them together, across the lake, he was buying them ice creams, his wife was taking a photo. I think they live in Leeds now, I saw his name in the Guardian last year, an article about his photographs . . . (*Pause.*) It was a very cold winter after you were born. There were power cuts. I couldn't keep the room warm; there were no lights in the tower blocks; I knew he had an open fire, it was trendy; so we took a bus to Didsbury, big gardens, pine kitchens, made a change from concrete. I rang the bell. (*Stops.*) A Punjabi man answered, said he was sorry . . . they'd moved. By the time we got back to Mosside it was dark, the lift wasn't working – (*Stops.*) That was the night I phoned Mummy. (*Difficult.*) Asked her. (*Pause.*) I tried! I couldn't do it, Rosie. (*Pause.*) It doesn't matter how much you succeed afterwards, if you've failed once. (*Pause.*) After you'd gone . . . I kept waking in the night to feed you . . . A week . . . in the flat . . . Then I went back to art school. Sandra and Hugh thought I was inhuman. I remember the books that came out that winter – how to succeed as a single working mother – fairytales! (*Pause.*) Sandra and Hugh have a family now. Quite a few of my friends do. (*Pause.*) I could give you everything now. Rosie? . . .

Rosie (*pause*) I used to hate you, only I never knew why. (*Gestures.*) Sit down on the swing. I'm going to Oldham, to live with Gran – Great-Gran. Dad says I can.

Jackie (*hesitates*) I'm frightened.

Rosie Sit down on the swing (*She holds the ropes.*) Put your head back and look up through the cherry tree. The sky is falling. Mum used to sit here with me in her arms, and I'd pretend I was asleep. I'm never having any children. (*Starts towards the house.*)

Jackie You might.

Rosie *hears, but keeps walking away.*

Lights fade to blackout.

Scene Six

The Wasteground.

Margaret *walks in, balancing on cracks of paving.*

Margaret King of the Golden River! (*Demonstrates invisible line.*) I'm the King.

Jackie (*runs in*) Farmer Farmer, may I cross your golden river, just to take our Daddy's dinner.

Jackie *runs to cross the line,* **Margaret** *chases and catches her.*

Margaret You've got to do a dare . . . !

Jackie I've been in the boys' den . . .

Margaret And?

Jackie They wanted me to kill you.

Margaret It didn't work.

Jackie Sure?

Margaret Yes.

Slight pause.

Jackie The others won't play with me any more.

Margaret Tell you what.

Jackie What?

Margaret You can come with me. To my secret, secret hide.

Margaret *holds out her hand.* **Jackie** *takes it.*

Jackie No. Not yet. Do you mind?

Margaret *shakes her head.* **Jackie** *lets go of her hand and walks away. The lights start to fade on* **Margaret,** *who stands watching until* **Jackie** *is out of sight.* **Margaret** *resumes balancing along the cracks in the paving. The lights fade to blackout during:*

Margaret King of the Golden River . . . I'm the King.

Scene Seven

Oldham, September 1987. The backyard of Doris's end terrace cottage. Distant sound of children. Two deck chairs. Piano stool from Act One, on it the Solitaire board from Act Two. A tub of geraniums. A green kite. Rosie is sunbathing in shorts and painted tee shirt, both of which she has tie-dyed herself, and she is wearing Walkman headphones, oblivious of all other noise. She hums 'Holding Back The Years', as she concentrates on the Solitaire game.

Doris (*appears upstage, holding up kite tail. Calls*) Is this right?

Rosie (*hums*) . . . Holding back the years . . .

Doris (*comes nearer*) Rosie? CAN YOU HEAR ME DEAR? (*Taps Rosie on the shoulder.*)

Rosie SORRY! (*Removes headphones.*)

Doris You're shouting again, dear. Neighbours will think I'm deaf. (*Holds up kite tail.*) Is this right?

Rosie Looks great! Thanks. (*Picks up the kite.*) Here, just tie it on the bottom.

Doris (*ties the kite tail to the kite*) Needs a stitch in it . . .

Rosie (*holds the kite aloft*) What d'you think?

Doris (*pause*) I preferred the blue ones.

Rosie Well they've ordered fifty, so I'm not complaining. (*Puts the kite down.*) Did ten this morning.

Doris I gathered that, from the state of the box room. Bits of string . . .

Rosie It's not for you to clear up. Sit down Doris, enjoy the sun.

Doris (*sits*) I fancy one of those garden tables . . . white ones, with an umbrella. But they do cost, don't they?

Rosie (*firmly*) When I've sold the next batch, maybe. We mustn't spend before we've paid off the overheads.

Doris You shouldn't be bothering your head with work on your birthday. (*Pause.*) Just like your mother.

Rosie Did you see her present!

Doris Mrs W saw me take it in. Postman couldn't get it through the letterbox.

Rosie It's one of her paintings.

Doris I propped it on the mantelpiece.

Rosie What d'you think?

Doris (*pause*) I liked the gold frame. Looks expensive.

Rosie Gran! She did it specially for me.

Rosie *returns to Solitaire.*

Doris Is Jackie still seeing that man with the hairdo?

Rosie Dreadlocks. You mean Andy, yeah. Think he's okay.

Doris D'you think she'll marry?

Rosie Last time I was with them they bought a duvet. They go shopping together.

Doris Like us.

Rosie You promised you'd show me how to do the Solitaire, today.

Doris You work it out. (*She watches* **Rosie** *for a moment.*) No cheating, mind. Took my Mother years to work it out. She showed me, but she made me vow never to tell anyone. I didn't even tell Jack, and husbands and wives aren't supposed to have any secrets, are they?

Rosie Listen, I've been trying all week, and I can't do it.

Doris One week is nothing.

Rosie *studies the board.*

Isn't this sunshine cheering? (*She puts on a pair of mirrored sunglasses.*)

Rosie What do you think my next move should be?

Doris What do you think, Rosie?

Rosie (*laughs*) Oh Doris, take my shades off!

Doris They're mine. Bought them at the checkout when I went for the ice cream.

Rosie There's a new Pakistani shop opened. Even cheaper than Kwiksave.

Doris Jack came home one night and I was sat in the dark. I told him, I'm economising. He said, that's just as well, you left the hall light on. (*Pause.*) You can't win.

Rosie You can. Look, double jump! Is that allowed?

Doris Yes. Do you know, I think I'll even take my stockings off, and then my legs can brown. (*Modestly reaches under her skirt and unhooks her stockings.*) Well, I may be as old as the Queen Mother, but *I* buy all my smalls in Top Shop.

Rosie Hmmm . . . (*Removes another marble.*)

Doris Do you know Rosie, there's no such snob as the snob who rises from the gutter . . .

Rosie Are you 'casting aspersions' again? Grubbing at the Royal Family this time, are you?

Doris No. As a matter of fact I was making an inference to my late husband. Jack would never have tolerated this lack of modesty in a woman. (*Pause.*) Although while we're on the subject, it is true that the Queen Mother was a Commoner before she married up.

Rosie AH! Triple jump! Fucking brill!

Doris Does one have to lower the tone of the afternoon quite so crudely?

Rosie Stop attempting posh, Doris. Your slip is showing.

Doris Is it? . . . Still, I don't suppose the Queen Mother does all her own washing . . . (*Leans back and closes her eyes.*)

Rosie *puts headphones back on. Hums.*

A lull.

Doris I suppose now you've got hold of that game, I won't be hearing from you till the Christmas after next.

Rosie (*singing softly. Moves a marble*) Ah!

Doris (*opens her eyes*) What with that electronic earmuff you wear, night and day.

Rosie (*studying the board*) Hmm . . .

Doris In my day, families practised the art of conversation.

Rosie Aah! (*Removes another marble.*)

Doris (*watches* **Rosie** *fondly*) Your mother couldn't solve that. Though she tried.

Rosie (*removes headphones*) Are you talking to me? (*Stretches.*) Mmm! It's hot, like being inside a blue balloon. (*Gazes out.*) The moors are clear today. We should've walked up to the Waterloo Memorial.

Doris (*gazes out*) Wicked, sticking these tower blocks in the view.

Rosie It's so lovely here, Doris. (*Pause.*) Ken phoned to say happy birthday. I asked him to put some flowers on Margaret's grave today.

Doris (*pause*) To think, Jack and I in this same street, 60 years ago – scrimping and saving so that our child would have a better start in life . . . You do what you believe is best for your daughter, you know Rosie, and then you find it wasn't what she wanted. Or needed.

Rosie Remember what Jackie said afterwards. We mustn't live in the past.

Doris Well I don't see that I've much of a future. Stuck here with my great-granddaughter in a two-up, two-down.

Rosie Gran!

Doris (*winding her up*) Forced to do piecework, tying scraps of coloured paper to lengths of string all day long . . .

Rosie How much do you want that garden table . . . ?

Doris You fancy you can bribe your great-grandmother?

Rosie Yes.

Doris (*pause*) How many did you say you wanted?

Rosie Fifty. By the end of the week. We can do them sitting out here.

Doris 'Campaign Kites' . . . Who'd have thought you'd earn a living off them. (**Rosie** *moves another marble.*) Who are they for this time?

Rosie Greenpeace.

Doris Had another phone call from that Animal Liberation man.

Rosie I won't do business with organisations that use violence. (*Pause.*) What did you tell him?

Doris That he was politically unsound.

Rosie That's a good phrase.

Doris Heard a girl say it at the evening class.

Rosie Let me guess . . . Tricia?

Doris No – a new girl in Women's Literature – She's from the tower block over there. I've met her in the Welfare with her two babbies, and do you know, she doesn't look the sort to even open a book. But she's quite the best, the comments she comes out with in class. She can't spell, of course. (*Pause.*) But it just goes to show: you can't judge by appearances. Jack was wrong. (*Pause.*) Even so, I do wish you wouldn't wear those dirty rags. You look . . . like a victim.

Rosie I made this tee shirt. It got ripped at the last march. Perhaps someone will find it in our cellar one day, and remember. (*Pause.*) And remember me.

Doris At least you're not wounded inside.

Pause.

Rosie (*removes another marble*) . . . Look, this is a magic marble: when you hold it up to the sun there's a frozen fountain inside.

Doris It seems no time since you were trying to push that up your nose. (*Pause.*) I'm going to put our tea on. Can you pass my shoes?

Rosie I'll do it.

Doris No, it really is my turn.

Rosie – Have you got me a birthday cake!

Doris Yes.

Rosie I love you, Doris.

Doris A long time since anyone's said that to me. (*Pause.*) Sixty-one years, Jack and I were married. I don't think we liked each other very much. (*Pause.*) There's a letter here for you.

Rosie There's no address on it.

Doris It's from your mother. I've kept it safe in my scrapbox, with Jack's letters, and Margaret's exercise book, and the drawings Jackie did when she was a little girl. (*Pause.*) After Margaret took you to London, Jackie came to see me. Left some baby clothes, and asked me to give you this letter when you reached sixteen. Happy Birthday. (*Kisses* **Rosie**. *Goes in to the cottage.*)

Rosie *picks up the letter, opens it and reads.*

Rosie '. . . I don't know if you'll ever love me as much as I love you. But one day you'll understand why I've done this to you, probably not until you are on your own yourself . . .' (**Rosie** *throws the letter down. After a moment she retrieves it. She concentrates on the Solitaire board and completes the game with a few last moves, so that one marble is left in the centre hole.*) Solitaire! (*Calls.*) Gran! Gran, guess what, I've discovered the secret, all by myself! Gran? I'll prove it to you, come and watch, I'm going to do it all over again now, so that I remember it always. You there Gran? (*Silence.*) Oh never mind.

Rosie *puts the headphones back on and hums quietly. As she replaces all the marbles on the board,* **Jackie** *appears upstage, dressed as in Act Three, Scene Five.* **Margaret** *appears also, dressed* *as in Act Three, Scene Two. The blue kite flies up high over* **Margaret.**

Scene Eight

Enter **Doris** *in the 1920s print dress which* **Jackie** *pulled from the box in Act Two and a straw hat trimmed with flowers. She is breathless and her hair is awry. Oldham, May 1923.*

Doris Mother! Mother? Oh, what do you think! It's happened, happened to me! All the way back on the train I could hardly keep still; I don't know what the other passengers must've thought, but I wouldn't be ladylike. Mother! Come and look. Do I look different? I must look different, I feel as though I've swallowed a firework. Oh it was a lovely, lovely day. We took a picnic, climbed up to the Waterloo Memorial, sat in the sunshine and it was after we'd finished the egg and cress; he couldn't wait till after the fruit cake! I felt so – shy, suddenly – I had to just stare and stare at the tablecloth while he was asking, blue and yellow squares, there was an ant struggling to carry a piece of cress across the corner . . . These are things you remember all your life, I suppose. I didn't think it would be like this. (*Pause.*) And then we just ran and ran! Talked, made plans, I felt somehow – weedy! (*Laughs.*) – Sort of silly, for having given in . . . to – love! – Do you know what I mean? (*Silence.*) Mother? We ate your fruit cake on the train. Jack put a paper down so as not to drop crumbs on the velvet upholstery, but then he sat on a strawberry – and oh, I got a grass stain on my frock, but Jack says he'll buy me a new one. *And*, Mother, *and* I got promoted to Head of Infants this morning! Miss Butterworth called me into her office, my heart was in my mouth, I thought she was going to tick me off for this dress being too short! . . . Jack was very proud when I told him, but of course he says I shan't need to work when we're – when we're – oh, of course he's going to ask you first, he's waiting in the front room, I opened the curtains so the neighbours can see – Oh and – (*Lights begin to fade.*) I've seen just the posy, tiny white flowers, in the window of Ambleton's . . . Oh Mother, I'm so happy, SO HAPPY! I suppose, really and truly, this is the beginning of my life! (*Lights fade to a single spot on* **Doris,** *then snap out.*)

Solution to the Solitaire Game

For Rosie in Act Three, Scene Seven.

A Solitaire board (see diagram on p. 95) looks much like a round wooden bread board, with a groove running round just inside the rim where discarded marbles are put. There are thirty-three holes on the board. Initially these are all filled with marbles except for the centre hole which is empty. The game is to clear the board leaving one marble in the centre hole. The rule is that a marble can only be moved by hopping it over another marble, up or down or across but not diagonally. The static marble which has been hopped over, is then removed from its hole and discarded.

For the scene, Rosie only needs the last eleven marbles on the board. She can then pace the final moves through the scene with Doris. There are no numbers on a Solitare board, but the diagram has been numbered for clarity. As can be seen, the following holes have marbles in them: five, nine, eleven, fifteen, seventeen, nineteen, twenty-one, twenty-two, twenty-four, twenty-six, twenty-seven.

The ten moves are as follows and each marble that is hopped over is removed from the board, while the hopping marble lands in a new hole.

   1. Marble from *twenty-one* jumps over marble in *twenty-two* and into hole *twenty-three*
   2. Marble from *twenty-seven* jumps over marble in *twenty-six* and into hole *twenty-five*
   3. Marble from *twenty-four* jumps over marble in *twenty-three* and into hole *twenty-two*
   4. Marble from *twenty-two* jumps over marble in *fifteen* and into hole *eight*
   5. Marble from *eight* jumps over marble in *nine* and into hole *ten*
   6. Marble from *ten* jumps over marble in *eleven* and into hole *twelve*
   7. Marble from *twelve* jumps over marble in *nineteen* and into hole *twenty-six*
   8. Marble from *twenty-six* jumps over marble in *twenty-five* and into hole *twenty-four*

9. Marble from *twenty-four* jumps over marble in *seventeen* and into hole *ten*

10. Marble from *five* jumps over marble in *ten* and into hole *seventeen*

The marble for the third move (from hole twenty-four) continues hopping through the next six moves. Therefore, when Rosie says 'double jump' or 'triple jump', what she is doing is playing the third to seventh moves as a sequence. The actress can delay picking up the hopped over marbles each time so as to prolong these moves. The stage directions indicate (*She removes a marble.*) every so often, as a rough guide. The actress can pace it as she wants, and add extra marbles if she wants more moves. At the point Doris leaves Rosie with the letter, Rosie should have four marbles left on the board, ready for the eighth, ninth and tenth moves. These are the moves with which Rosie completes the game alone and ends with one marble in the centre hole – seventeen. Solitaire!

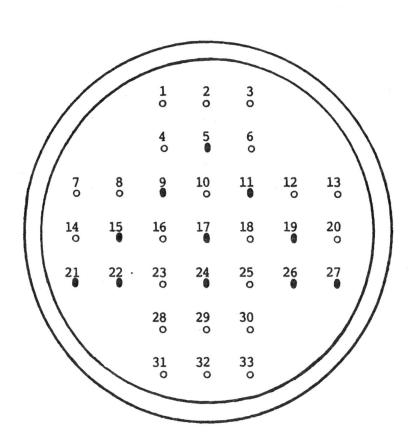

Appendix: Practical Exercises

Exercises exploring themes and conventions of the play, for practical
study or towards a performance.

Children/Adults: Exercise 1

Use a large space. Ask the group to move freely around the room:
run, jump, and shake out the body. Every so often a command is
called (see below for examples). In between these commands,
continue moving about as actively as possible. Give a few moments
to each command, for each individual to find the body shape. Ask
the members of the group to hold these and feel their strength,
emotions, and potential for action. This can be done silently or
aloud.

Command: become a very frightened child
  e.g. Margaret in Act One, Scene Two
  e.g. Jackie in Act Three, Scene Three
Command: become a very frightened adult
  e.g. Margaret in her office, Act Three, Scene Two
  e.g. Jackie in Act Three, Scene Five
Command: become a very angry child
  e.g. Rosie burying Suky, Act One, Scene Ten
Command: become a very angry adult
  e.g. Doris in Act One, Scene Two
Command: become a child showing love
  e.g. Jackie at the end of Act One, Scene Two
Command: become an adult showing love
  e.g. Jackie in Act One, Scene Six

Afterwards, discuss which parts of the body were used to react and
communicate, as a child and as an adult. Where was emotion or
tension held in the body?

Actors find that the child scenes allow them to re-charge energy
during the play, and release some of the stress of the adult scenes.
Try moving from an adult to a child pose and back again. Split the
group into audience and performers to observe this.

As the audience, notice when the state of the person is

externalised and when it is internalised. Which shapes would most make you want to watch the play and find out what is happening?

Try moving from one adult state to another adult state, through anger, fear, love and grief. How does this look to the audience, and how does this feel to the actor?

Exercise 2

Ask students to sit or stand as themselves in the study group, and then to notice how they present themselves. Now ask them to find the internal child voice and listen to its desires; to run out of the room, shout, eat, go and play with or fight another person. Express the child in a group improvisation, or by writing down the internal voice. Try drawing a picture of the child inside the adult, and assemble these to reveal the oldest group of people in the room.

Exercise 3

Ask the group to move freely around the space. Ask them to visualise and then become the oldest person they have ever met. Spend some moments finding this physically. Ask the group members for words describing their feelings, energy and potential for action. Move freely around the room again. Stop and become a young person in love. Find the physical image for this. Ask the participants to describe their feelings, energy and potential for action. Move freely around the room again. Stop and become the old person, but this time imagine you are in love. How does the child appear in the adult? How does this person feel? Which image of a person is more interesting and dramatic?

Exercise 4

In small groups, choose a section of a child scene where a game explores what it is to be a girl or a woman, experiencing sexual desire, childbirth, menstrual pain or the sexual advances of a man. Find the physical image suggested by the dialogue for each of these. Show these to the group. Are these funny? If people laugh, what are they laughing at? Do these moments feel funny to perform?

Look at how these compare with the images produced by adults in the play.

Exercise 5: Structure

Ask each member of a group to think of the three or four most important events in their life so far. These should be events fixed at one moment in time, such as birth or death of a family member, start of a new school, moving home, learning a skill, winning or losing a prize, meeting a significant person.

Write down three or four such events quickly, without thinking about why you have chosen them. Simply list them in the order of importance. Ask people to read out their lists. Observe whether the order of importance is also the order of conventional chronology.

Exercise 6: Light

Assemble as many different sources of light as possible: candles, torches, overhead bulbs, fluorescent striplights, natural light from windows and the possibility for blacking out the room you are in. Set up each kind of light in turn and improvise a situation. Observe how the volume of words spoken, the action and energy of the characters, changes each time.

If you have a studio with a stage lighting rig, set up some of the lighting for scenes in *My Mother Said I Never Should* and act out a passage. Change the lighting and try the passage again. For example, put Act Three, Scene Three into bright day; Act Three, Scene Seven under a cold winter sky.

Exercise 7: Colour

In a large space ask a group to move freely around, and then, when the name of a colour is called, to freeze into a shape suggested by that colour. Observe the size and energy of these shapes, and which part of the body responds most to each colour. Do people in the group produce similar shapes? Does this set up an atmosphere in the room? Continue the exercise with different primary colours. Afterwards, discuss the emotions or energy which people experienced as they became each colour. Do some colours feel more feminine, or masculine?

Exercise 8: Environment

Ask everybody to stand along one side of the room you are in, abandoning their chairs, books, coats and anything else being used in the room. Announce that the group has arrived in a theatre to see a play, so it is now looking at the environment as it is set up for the beginning of the play. Discuss what kind of play is suggested by the set. Does it look like a comedy, farce, or political play? Does it look as if the structure will be one or three acts, or forty short scenes? Decide on the size of the cast. Are they women or men, how old, and what is their occupation? Where have they gone, or where will they arrive from? Invent the plot. Is the outside world visible? What kind of lighting or sound is there? Look for suspicious objects or costumes. Is this a boring or exciting play and does the set make you want to know what happens next?

Exercise 9: Objects

Ask everybody to bring an object to the session. This should be an object which reminds them of an important event in their lives. Display all the objects on the floor. Ask each person to tell the story attached to the object, explaining how the object was used, broken or touched during the real event. Once all the stories have been told, put several objects together and have a small group improvise a scene using the objects, while the rest of the group watches.

Ask a second group to take on the same characters and improvise another scene, using the same objects. In the second scene, the events of the first scene can be referred to – but only in the way objects are placed or used, not through words.

Discuss how many of the objects people have brought in are ones which everybody uses and recognises. Are some objects intrinsically funny, or threatening? In other words, do some objects have a character – and can we change this?

Exercise 10: Costume

Ask everybody to bring to the session an item of women's or girls' clothing from any period of the twentieth century. This can include shoes. Arrange the outfits in a row on the floor, in chronological order. Describe the kind of woman suggested by each costume; her personality, sense of humour, sexiness, manners and occupation. Decide how many of these outfits could be worn by one woman through her life.

Distribute the clothes among the group, and try them on. How does it feel to walk, run, sit down and get up again, or dance, wearing this costume? Are there some activities you could *not* do? Decide on the age of the woman who wears this outfit. For whom is she wearing this costume?

Exercise 11: Dance

Divide a large group into small groups of four, three, two or one, and allocate to each a scene of the play. Give each group some minutes to explore its scene, finding the amount of space and action it needs to use by playing the scene (NOT from standing about discussing it). The full text of the scene need not be read aloud. The focus is on finding the dance of the scene: the body sizes and heights, the space between them, the work or play of the scene. After several runs, ask each group to show its scene to the rest of the group by performing the dance only, without the words.

Ask the audience to discuss what it can see about the scene from the dance alone. Can you tell the age and status of characters; who is a parent; their feelings about themselves and each other; the purpose of their meeting?

Ask each group to select the moment in the dance which they feel sums up the meaning of the scene. This might be the opening or closing image, or one during the scene. Ask the groups to freeze this moment, paying attention to details of the dance. Look at each scene image. Ask the frozen statues to describe their feelings in that position. Compare this to the lines of dialogue they speak. The dance enacts the subtext of the scene, and in this way many themes are performed.

Set out the dance of the whole play by arranging the groups in the order of the scenes, with each group held in its frozen image. Look at the number of women in each scene. Look at where and when the women are standing or sitting. Do they ever sit together? What does this dance of the play tell the audience? How often does a scene end with one woman alone? Is this person a mother or daughter and who does she need or want?

Exercise 12: Language

Most of my time writing is spent thinking out how the situation feels for a character, and then asking myself questions about the characters for whom I am writing dialogue. This process can be enacted.

As a playwright, write one of the following:

Jackie's telephone call to Margaret, telling her about Rosie (see Act One, Scene Six)

or: Rosie's postcard from Venice, to Margaret (see Act Three, Scenes One and Two)

or: Jackie's letter to Rosie written when Rosie was a baby (see Act Three, Scene Seven).

Read these aloud.

Now set up the environment in which the character, rather than the playwright, first writes or speaks these words. The playwright should now spend some moments finding the physical circumstances and age of the character. Other players should become the two or three other women in the situation. The playwright now reads aloud what she/he has written, with the following included:

For Jackie's telephone call to Margaret, have Rosie and Doris interrupt with their own opinions and questions about their future roles.

For Rosie's postcard, have Margaret and Jackie talk to Rosie about what is happening in their lives.

For Jackie's letter, have Rosie ask the details of how she will be brought up, and Margaret tell Jackie her hopes for Jackie.

Compare the two versions of the scene. Look at any difference in vocabulary, style, sentence structure and imagery in the writing.

Glossary

This glossary is intended for use by overseas students as well as by English-born readers.

16 *A.B.C.* – the name of a chain of cafes in England.

41 *abstract* – a style of painting based on theory rather than trying to represent figures or landscape.

10 *Anderson Shelter* – an air raid shelter like a steel box, small enough to be set up in the room of a house, and used during the Second World War in Britain.

55 *anorak* – children's waterproof jacket, usually with a hood.

88 *aspersions* – doubts, of a slanderous or disapproving kind.

31 *Austin Healey* – type of car, new and racy in the 1950s; some models have a pull down soft-top roof.

69 *backyard* – small, stone flagged (paved) yard the width of a terraced house and about 5 m. long, originally for hanging out washing and for outside lavatory; usually separated from adjacent backyards by walls, with a door in the bottom wall to a communal alley running between two rows or terraces of small houses.

61 *beehive* – women's hairstyle of the 1950s, where the hair is piled high on the head, and hairspray, or a mixture of sugar and water, is used to stiffen the hair and give it body.

59 *bicarb* – abbreviation for bicarbonate of soda, used as a raising agent when making scones.

44 *binliner* – large plastic refuse sack, usually black, used for outside dustbins rather than in the house.

24 *black ice* – thin, smooth ice on the road which is dangerous because it cannot be seen.

42 *Blu-tac* – soft putty for sticking posters or pictures to walls.

11 *bolster* – old-fashioned sausage-shaped pillow, firmly stuffed.

49 *brill* – abbreviation for brilliant, a key term of approval used by young people in the late-1980s.

72 *cappucino* – frothy, milky coffee made in the Italian manner.

17 *carrier* – or carrier bag; plastic disposable shopping bag from supermarkets.

41 *choc-a-bloc* – idiom for crowded, when things or people are jostling for space.

77 *conkers* – the nuts of the horse chestnut tree.

37 *creeping* – Lancashire idiom for walking slowly or being frail.

47 *crockery* – china ware or earthenware.

15 *curse* – women's slang for the menstrual period; the euphemism meant periods could be mentioned in front of children or men, without embarrassment – but with some mystery.

57 *Cynth* – abbreviation for Cynthia, popular English girls' name in the first part of the twentieth century.

49 *duvet* – modern quilt which does not need a sheet under it.

59 *elbow* – short for 'elbow grease', meaning arm power; as when Doris says she used 'just elbow', not bicarb, to make her scones rise.

47 *end terrace* – end house in a row or terrace of houses joined together, usually nineteenth-century workers' housing.

14 *fairy cakes* – cup cakes; individual round iced cakes in paper cases, often made for children's parties.

45 *flask* – abbreviation for thermos flask, an insulated screw–top jug for keeping drinks hot on picnics.

23 *flat* – English word for an apartment, a home on one or sometimes two floors of a house or tower block.

14 *formica* – brand name for a tough plastic surface invented for kitchens, counters and tables in the late 1950s.

11 *gas mask* – a rubber mask covering the face, with a filter over the mouth to protect against poisonous gases; all British children were issued with one during World War Two.

52 *goitre* – enlargement of the thyroid gland visible as a swelling at the front of the neck.

72 *gondola* – flat-bottomed boat traditional for transport on the canals of Venice, now mostly used for tourist trips.

5 *gypsies* – ancient nomadic race possibly originating in Egypt, who brought their language and culture into Europe, including songs, dances and the ability to see into the future.

10 *Hallé orchestra* – famous symphony orchestra of Manchester.

60 *hippy* – late 1960s–early 1970s follower of anti-establishment music and fashion; their practices included sex outside marriage, smoking dope, wearing colourful loose clothes and beads, and long hair for men and women.

24 *holdall* – roomy zip-topped bag for clothes or household goods.

15 *hoola hoop* – plastic hoop which gave its name to 1960s game of spinning the hoop fast and continuously around the waist.

88 *inference* – a deduction; Doris possibly confuses the word with reference.

22 *iron tablets* – vitamin pills to boost the iron in the blood especially after illness or blood loss.

42 *kazooming* – zooming, going very fast, almost out of control.

22 *Kendal mint cake* – bar of peppermint and sugar invented in the Lake District town of Kendal, to give energy to hillwalkers.

9 *knickers* – girls' underpants; in Margaret's generation these were large and baggy compared to modern knickers.

14 *larder* – food storage cupboard large enough to walk into, lined with shelves on three sides.

84 *lift* – mechanical elevator carrying people between the floors of a tall building.

76 *May Bank holiday* – traditional day off work in the United Kingdom.

44 *mega* – slang for enormous, used by children in the late 1980s.

37 *mither* – pronounced my-ther – Lancashire idiom; a state of indecision, bother and worry.

24 *Moses basket* – soft straw basket with handles either side, used as a carrycot for a baby.

61 *outlaw* – illegal person, fugitive, usually because of crime.

22 *pampered* – treated with an indulgent amount of care.

10 *perseverance* – endurance under adversity to see a project through to its completion.

70 *persist* – to continue to try.

7 *piggy* – derogatory, slang term for someone who eats too much.

88 *posh* – elegant or wealthy in an ostentatious manner.

29 *rationing* – British Government policy during and after World War Two, to restrict food and clothing supplies to a certain amount per person per week.

78 *Red Star* – express overnight parcel delivery by rail between cities in Britain.

70 *redundant* – unemployed (of a person); unnecessary.

37 *revise* – to study intensively for an exam.

43 *rise* – a pay increase in the weekly wage.

57 *salver* – silver tray; used in respectable households in the nineteenth century, for visitors to put their calling card on when making social calls. Nowadays a decorative item often presented to a person to mark an event and inscribed with the signatures of colleagues.

49 *sardines* – a game of hide-and-seek, where one person hides and, as the others discover her or him, they squash into the same hiding place.

84 *scrimping* – idiom for making meals or clothes out of scraps of food or cloth, so as to save on household spending.

59 *scone* – small, dense tea cake served with butter or cream.

7 *séance* – group meeting to contact spirits, dead relatives.

88 *smalls* – idiom for underwear.

22 *smartie* – children's small chocolates coated with bright sugar colours, sometimes used to decorate cakes.

66 *solitaire* – traditional game for one player. (See pp. 92–4 for explanation and diagram.)

6 *split* – slang verb; to tell tales or expose someone.

70 *statistic* – Margaret refers to the social studies of numbers of the population whose marriages end in divorce, studies which were widely publicised through the 1980s.

60 *swinger* – 1960s slang jargon for a fashionable hippy who enjoys dancing.

57 *synth* – abbreviation for synthesizer, an electronic keyboard capable of synthesising the sound of any orchestral instrument; used by pop music bands in the 1980s.

13 *telly* – abbreviation for television.

23 *temping* – slang for a typing job as a temporary secretary on a short-term contract.

29 *threadbare* – cloth worn to the threads with no softness or pile remaining.

18 *transistor* – small portable radio in brightly coloured plastic, first cheaply available in the late 1960s.

89 *two-up two-down* – traditional northern working class housing, consisting of a front room and kitchen downstairs, and two bedrooms upstairs, with the lavatory originally in a privy in the stone flagged backyard.

69 *umbrage* – outrage and hurt pride, responding to a real or imagined insult.

13 *utility* – functional style of clothes, crockery and furniture designed in World War two to make a virtue of rationed. materials; utility ware was a greenish grey glazed dinner service, the mugs a plain cylinder, tapering slightly at the base.

 7 *voodoo* – a religious cult where the wishes of the participants can be put on an absent person; usually evil or good health is visited upon the named victim, who is represented in the ceremony by a doll, or pieces of their actual hair or teeth; the cult is ancient practice in Haiti and Africa, but only used among witches in Europe.

63 *wally* – mid-1980s slang for a foolish person.

 8 *wireless* – early household radio set, 1920s–1950s, run on batteries.

55 *yucky* – unpleasant.

Questions for Further Study

1. Who do you think is the central character in the play and why?
2. If the characters were animals, what kind of animals do you think they would be?
3. What role do the male characters have in the play?
4. Instead of four generations, would the play be better showing three or five generations?
5. Which character would you choose to act and what is it that appeals to you about her? How would you prepare to play the role?
6. How many plays do you know with an all-female cast? When were they written? Why do you think this is?
7. The play ends in 1989. Staging the play now, what do you consider has changed and what remains the same?
8. What effect does the jumbled chronology of scenes have on the audience? How does the chronology affect the actors in the way they play each scene?
9. Is this a difficult play to design? What are the challenges? Describe or draw a design concept.
10. Why have the majority of new plays by women been produced in studio theatres not on larger stages? What size and shape stage would you choose for this play and why?
11. What does the play achieve and create that could not be done by television or film drama?
12. If you removed the child scenes from the play, what would happen to the story, suspense, humour and characters' journeys in the play as a whole?
13. Michael Attenborough, the director of the Royal Court première, described the play as 'the emotional highlights of the twentieth century'. What do you think he meant?
14. Max Stafford-Clark, artistic director of the Royal Court at the time, described the play as 'deeply political'. Discuss definitions of a political play.
15. How important to the meaning of the play is the physical action or work done by the women in each scene? How would you use this as a director?
16. Imagine you were auditioning actors; what qualities would you look

for in actors to play Doris, Margaret, Jackie and Rosie?

17. Discuss the differences and similarities in Doris and Rosie as characters and in the way they live their lives.
18. How much are Margaret and Jackie the product of their times or would their characters behave the same way in any generation?
19. Describe how you would use colour, sound and light in a production of this play. Is this a naturalistic play?
20. Comment on the differences in vocabulary, rhythm and humour in the characters and give examples.
21. Why is a play with an all-female cast assumed to be 'feminist' or mainly of interest to women, while a play with an all-male cast is seen as representing all human life? Is this changing?
22. Do you think it is the job of a playwright to invent new form as well as new content?
23. The play has been described as Brechtian in structure, Stanislavskian in the adult scenes and Artaudian in the child scenes. Explain how the theories of these practitioners cast light on the play.
24. *Top Girls* and *My Mother Said I Never Should* were written at the beginning and the end of the nineteen eighties. What are their parallels and differences?